Praise for the *Oh Daddy Ch*

"This tale will be retold for years to come. (r.r.)

"Here, here let us raise a glass of Clorox to the distinguished author." (F.P.)

"Awesome tract!" (E.W.)

"The pieces are well-written, entertaining, and excellent political satire." (former Senate Majority Leader Tom Daschle)

"Your mind works in mysterious ways." (E.T.)

"Whenever you send another episode, I just take a hydroxychloroquine and read on." (G.N.)

"Bravo. Your best one. I laughed out loud." (S.S.)

"sick, sick, sick, I love it." (D.P.)

"Just laughed my way out of Florida and into southern Georgia. "Oh Daddy" even made me forget I was hungry and needed a pit stop." (J.C.)

"You really need to find a hobby." (B.B.)

"I knew there was a reason for me not to opt out of receiving your hallucinogenic induced writings." (T.R.)

"They're entertaining. They're weird." (K.R.)

"You have a furtive imagination and a gift for the bizarre." (G.P.)

"Do not email me anymore." (J.G.)

"I like the culture thrown in with the foreign phrases, it makes me feel so sophisticated when I read it aloud." (F.P.)

"Super episode!" (E.W.)

"Provides amusement to start the day." (R.H.)

"Hilarious episode." (D.P.)

"I am delighted that you are spreading knowledge about quarks through your bizarre and imaginative story." (G.P.)

"OMG…Your brain is amazingly convoluted." (P.T.)

"Not sure if your brain may be a bit fried from all of this creative thinking, but it's my favorite episode yet!" (E.W.)

"It's hard to figure how your mind works." (E.W.)

OH DADDY
CHRONICLES

Print ISBN: 978-1-09833-388-1

eBook ISBN: 978-1-09833-389-8

DEDICATION

To my family, without whose wisdom, unwavering support
and encouragement, and occasional answering of the
phone when I call, this work would not be possible.

Here's to you – K, S, and S. That stands for kiss.

OH DADDY CHRONICLES

A Contemporary Political Satire

BARRY ROBBINS

TABLE OF CONTENTS

Fly on the Wall

"Oh daddy, I am not happy."

"I can see that dear. Your face is pouty. But that only makes me wish even more that you weren't my daughter so I could grab your pussy. Tell me what I can do to make my Snuzzlepuff happy again."

"It's Jared. He's so busy with all these important projects to save the world - peace in the Middle East, opioid epidemic, remaking government, coronavirus supply chains, figuring out how to economize on toothpaste by being able to put the excess that was squeezed out back into the tube. I see so little of him, including the part of him that is so little anyway. That really doesn't bother me much - after all, he is kind of a dumb dweeb. It's just that he gets to pretend that he is competent to do all sorts of things that, of course, he knows nothing about. I want in on the action."

"OK, let me give this some thought."

(Two seconds later.)

"I've got it! We'll form a new task force for the reopening of the economy."

"Sounds great. And I get to be on it? If Dr. Fauci is on it, can I sit next to him? He's just so cute I could..."

"No dear, not that task force. I want you to actually chair a new task force charged with an even more important mission."

"Oh boy, this sounds good. What is it that I could be even less qualified for?"

"A task force to plan and implement the big, beautiful, stupendous, magnificent, best in the world military parade to mark the opening of the economy. I want lots of tanks (tank you very much) and huge crowds. You might want to consult with Vladikins on this. He has a lot of experience."

"Oh daddy, you're the best. I can't wait to get started. I've already got an idea about having a separate parade section of COVID-19 people to show all the voters that even the people suffering as a direct result of your incompetence and archetypal narcissism plan to vote for you. Jared will be so jealous!"

(Snuzzlepuff comes over to Daddykins, throws her arms around him, then coughs and sneezes in his face.)

The Signing

"Oh daddy. What are you doing now?"

(Snuzzlepuff walks into the Oval Office and sees Daddykins behind the Resolute Desk resolutely massaging his right hand.)

"Hi dear. I'm busy violating the Hatch Act. Boy, I usually find election cheating to be so much fun, but this time it's a pain in the ass. If only my number one Jew boy Steve hadn't promised everyone they would have their $1200 checks so quickly. My hand really hurts signing my name on every one of these."

"I feel so sorry for you, Daddykins. But think of it this way. Every time you sign a check, imagine that you are sticking a pin under Crazy Nancy Pelosi's fingernails. Go ahead and try it."

(Big grin washes across Daddykin's face, but even ogling Snuzzlepuff doesn't generate any movement downstairs.)

"You know, maybe I could sign a few for you. After all, I'm also a worse than useless White House employee. And I could sign them in my own name - complete with curlicues and a cute heart over the "I." Could I have the batch going to 21 year old hunks?"

"Interesting idea, dear. Let me check with counsel."

(15 minutes later.)

"Rudy says it's OK, dear. He also said to make sure the check you send to Hunter Biden is for at least $100,000 so we can investigate him during the campaign season."

(After five minutes of laborious signing, Snuzzlepuff calls it a day, throws her arms around Daddykins and coughs and sneezes into his face.)

The Spreadsheet

"Oh daddy, I just looked at the most horrible spreadsheet I think I've ever seen."

"Calm down, Snuzzlepuff, I'm sure I can take care of things. After all, the President has all the authority the President has. But first, what is a spreadsheet? Is that what they call the bed covers in cheap motels?"

"Not really, daddy, it's sort of like a big chart with lots of numbers on it. But don't worry, this one comes from Microsoft, not that nasty little dweebie guy from Amazon."

"Where did you pick it up?"

"The virus? No, I don't think I picked it up. But if I did, it would have been during that trip I made to Bedminster in violation of your stay at home rules. Breaking rules is always so much fun and, I hope you don't mind my saying this, but breaking your rules is the most fun of all."

"Like father, like daughter. Anyway, tell me about this horrible spreadsheet thing."

"Well, you know how you are always bragging about how the U.S. has done a lot more tests than any other country in the world?"

"Of course, Muslims might pray six times a day, but I say the testing thing at least 19 times a day. That's because everyone wants to hear it over and over and over and over and... And not only the number of tests, but our tests are clearly the most beautiful and the most accurate and the most sexy and the most likely to win an Academy Award and maybe even a Golden Globe and they certainly have the highest ratings. You wouldn't believe how high their ratings are - unbelievable. No test has ever come close to these ratings. Number 2 on Facebook (behind me). Number 2 on Instagram (behind me). Number..."

(Snuzzlepuff interrupts because she is getting hungry.)

"So, daddy, this is what that yucky spreadsheet says:"

Number of SARS-CoV-2 tests per 1000 of population, as of April 16, 2020:

Iceland - 109.56

UAE - 77.55

Luxembourg - 50.58

Norway - 24.02

Switzerland - 23.85

Israel - 21.63

Germany - 20.63

Spain - 19.90

Qatar - 19.57

Italy - 19.49

Australia - 14.90

Denmark - 14.22

Canada - 12.39

Belgium - 11.59

Russia - 11.06

South Korea - 10.52

United States - 9.97

Finland - 8.97

The Netherlands - 8.63

United Kingdom - 6.15

Turkey - 6.14

France - 5.11

Iran - 3.69

"So what do you think, daddy?"

(Daddy spends the next three seconds deep in thought.)

"Well, the high numbers in Spain and Italy prove that if you test a lot, you get a lot of people who die. This clearly vindicates my strategy of ignoring things. As to Luxembourg, UAE, Qatar - never heard of them. And why isn't Qatar spelled Quatar; even I know that q must always be followed by u. Regarding Germany, I never did like that Merkel (Merkel? Merkle? Murkle? Murrkklle?) person - too frumpy and thoughtful. And I also never did like those young upstarts who think that speaking French makes them sound sexy and intelligent -Trudeau and Macron(oni). Although I think I might need to change my mind about Macron(oni.)

"OK, good analysis. But what do we do now?"

"Same thing we always do - make up whatever reality we want and sell it to those baskets of deplorables - hook, line, and stinker."

(Snuzzlepuff comes over to Daddykins, puts her arms around him and coughs and sneezes into his face.)

(Just then, the door opens and in walks Danko, aka Don Jr. The plot thickens.)

Chip Off the Old Block

(Danko, aka Don Jr., enters the Oval Office to see his father sitting resolutely behind the Resolute Desk playing with one of those thingies where you pull one ball from the end and let it smash against the others causing the opposite end ball to swing. There is a look of awe and perplexity on daddy's face. He almost doesn't notice the entry of the son that bears his name.)

"Hi Popsicle. What's shaking down today?"

"Danko, you know I have asked you many times not to use that intellectual type of speech. I just don't understand it. Talk plain and stupid like everyone else in the Trump family."

"Duh, okay. I was just hankerin' to stop in and say howdy to my dada and to brag about how well I pulled off that assignment you gave me."

"Yes, by all accounts, it looks to have been a huge, beautiful success. How did you go about organizing it?"

"I got some of those wacko right-wing neo-Nazi types with which you have a mutual admiration society relationship, mixed in some Ted Kaczynski devotees, along with some new friends we made in Charlottesville and, to top it off, got libertarian Rand Paul to scrounge up some people who are even nuttier than he is. And, voilà, it all came together."

"Ted Kaectisocinki?"

"The Unabomber, dad."

"Oh, yeah. Him. (Dad scratches his head with a perplexed look on his Cheetos dusted face.)

"Anyway, son, what did you think of your old man's coup de grace - the LIBERATE tweets? Put a nice finishing touch on the groundwork you laid eh?"

"Sure did. I learned from the best. And you know what is even better? I was able to recruit all those people by promising them they would receive a check for $1200 with your name on it. Gotta give credit where it's due - nice going Stevie Jew boy."

"Just one thing, son. Do not get overconfident. Stay under the radar. Remember what happened to Uncle Paul and Uncle Roger. Don't get caught!"

"Good advice, popsicle."

"Before you go, tell me how you and that girlfriend of yours are doing. What's her name - Kimberly Gargoyle?"

"Guilfoyle, dad."

"Gilligan?"

"Guilfoyle, dad."

"Drill for oil?"

"GUILFOYLE, dad, G-U-I-L-F-O-Y-L-E."

"Ok, ok, whatever. As long as you like her and can take some of her money. But I really am not convinced she's your type."

"Why not?"

"Well, she just seems smart, that's all."

(Danko storms out of the Oval Office, slamming the door behind him. Daddy goes back to playing with his ball swinging thingy.)

To Test or not to Test

"Oh daddy. I just heard the terrible news. I'm so upset."

"What terrible news is that, Snuzzlepuff? There are so many horrible things these days that I'm responsible for. Of course, I take absolutely no responsibility for any of these things, but I make up for it by taking credit for all three things that have gone well... OK, maybe it's only two things...or one...or almost one. Anyway. You were saying."

"Yes. I just found out that that awful Navy guy tested positive for coronavirus!"

"You mean my valet? The job title that rhymes with pallet and mallet and almost with salad?"

"That's the hunk, I mean nasty man. And what's more, Danko says he has found out that it's all part of a Deep State plot to kill you. It seems that the hunk, I mean valet, is actually the bastard son of Nancy Pelosi and George Conway. Danko got all this from his girlfriend Kimberly Gargoyle who got it from Laura Ingraham at Fox News who got it from Dr. Oz who got it from Steve Bannon who got it from your spiritual advisor Paula White who got it in a daytime reverie while taking a shit from eating too many tacos on Taco Tuesday."

"Damn. And now I might get it. But wait a minute, the valet is black and Crazy Nancy and Scumbag George are both white."

"Yes. Now you see just how ingenious these Deep State plotters are and the lengths to which they will go to deceive you. But what are you going to do about the situation?"

"Don't worry. I've already taken care of things. First, I figured out how to use this to my advantage. I've created a new White House Office of the Scumbags and Chief of Staff Meadows has assigned this group a small, cramped office in a remote corner of the White House basement. Assigned to this unventilated office are Fiona Hill, Ambassador Bill Taylor, Ambassador Marie Yagjjthbvihfovich, Lt. Colonel Vindman, and all the inspectors general that I've fired and plan to fire. I told Mark we might need a bigger office, but he still has to keep it small, stuffy, and cramped. And, what is so great about the current situation, is that I have assigned the sick, coughing, sneezing, wheezing valet (who, as an added bonus, is a touchy feely guy) to that very same room. It's also a mask free zone. But I'm not a total ogre. Outside the room, ready for use, are two of the non-ventilator ventilators that Musk provided."

"You certainly are clever, daddy, but I'm still worried about your safety. That super cutie dootie Dr. Fauci Wauci says that COVID-19 is likely to be really nasty in people over 70 (you) and with comorbid conditions. (He's just so sexy when he talks like that. Jared never does, the dweeb.) The conditions usually mentioned include diabetes, high blood pressure, obesity and heart problems. I am concerned for you if having little or no heart and being congenitally stupid are also risk factors."

"Ah, I so appreciate your concern Snuzzlepuff. But once again, your very stable genius daddy has figured it out. I have demanded that I get a Chinese virus diagnostic test every day instead of once a week. So I'm protected!"

(At that moment, Dr. Fauci and Dr. Birx enter the Oval Office. Snuzzlepuff huddles with them in a corner of the room.)

"Oh daddy, I think your brilliant plan is not quite so brilliant. In fact, it demonstrates a total lack of understanding of this whole pandemic process that we have been living with."

"Huh?"

(Fauci and Birx explain.)

"You see, Mr. President, a diagnostic test does not, in any way, protect the person being tested. That is because we have no therapeutics against COVID-19 other than a modestly useful late stage antiviral. The diagnostic testing is to protect individuals who might come into contact with the tested person, not to protect the tested person himself."

"Aha! Thank you Dr. Fauci and Deborah. You have just vindicated the position I have taken from day one. Because getting tested doesn't help me, all testing is a waste of time and resources. You two can leave now."

(Fauci and Birx leave.)

"Anything else on your mind, Snuzzlepuff?"

"Well, actually, there is one thing and you're not going to like what I'm going to say."

"OK, out with it."

"About ten days ago, you had one of those press availability meetings here in the Oval Office. Stephen Hahn, Anthony Fauci, and Deborah Birx were present. I don't remember exactly what the topic was, but at some point in your remarks you referred to "Dr. Hahn, Dr. Fauci, and Deborah." I was totally offended."

"Offended? Whatever for?"

"The men were addressed as "Dr." The woman was addressed simply by her first name. The fact that she is a woman in no way diminishes the hard work, advanced knowledge, lifesaving skill set, academic achievements, and real-life commitment to applying her impressive abilities to helping others. She is as deserving of being addressed as "Dr." as are her esteemed colleagues, especially when mentioned in the same sentence and in their presence. Your behavior was repugnant. It was an affront to all women and you owe half of the human race an apology!"

"My goodness, Snuzzlepuff! I have never heard you speak in such an eloquent way!"

"I'm sorry, daddy. It's just that when I get angry like this, I forget who I'm talking to and might, therefore, forget to use simple words and short sentences."

"That's OK. I forgive you and I still have no idea what you were talking about."

"Achhhhhhhhhh!"

(Snuzzlepuff, now transformed into Ivanka, tears at her hair and storms out of the Oval Office.)

Who was that Masked Man?

(The scene shifts to a sitting room in the East Wing of the White House. The President and First Lady are sitting on a sofa. Melania gets up and moves to a chair on the other side of the room.)

"Why did you move? You're not doing that stupid social distancing thing on me, are you? You know, the only reason I agreed to that was to get that scarf lady Birx to stop nagging. All she did was nag. Nag. Nag. Nag. Social distance. Social distance. Social distance. Meeeeeee meeeeeeee meeeeee meeeeeee meeeeeeeeee. Drove me crazy. Typical female. I almost disbanded the task force because of that.

"On the other hand, I kind of like that Fauci guy. Even though I usually don't like people who are way smarter than I am ("Zat's vhy you have no friends, maybe?" interjected Melania), Tony's alright. He says what he thinks. And boy is he smart, especially for one of those Italian types. Good thing he didn't decide to open a pizza parlor like the rest of them.

"But you didn't answer my question - Why did you move to that chair?"

"Because you smell like my uncle Slobodan who is a pig farmer in Zagorje ob Savi."

"Do you miss Slovakia?"

"Vhy vould I miss Slovakia? I from Slovenia. Don't you know ze difference by now? Even Barron knows his geography and he is not ze sharpest tack in ze classroom, no?"

(Educational interjection: Melania Trump was born Melanija Knavs in Novo Mesto, Slovenia in 1970. She became a naturalized American citizen in 2006.)

"So now zat ze coronawirus is in ze Vite House, vill you now start vearing a mask to set an example?"

"Wear a mask? I'd sooner wear mascara. (President chortles at his cleverness with words.) "On the other hand, I guess I would wear mascara if only they made it in my shade of orange. But in answer to your "qvestion," I have no intention of ever wearing a mask because doing so would jeopardize my chances of re-election."

"Yes, and zis is so how?"

"I figure it like this. There is no way my supporters, my base, would ever wear a mask, even if I did. That means a bunch of them will die and take votes away from me in Florida, Michigan, Wisconsin, and Pennsylvania. On the other hand, if I don't wear a mask and downplay its importance, then some of Sleepy Joe's supporters will be tempted not to wear a mask and more of them will die, thus offsetting the loss of votes from my base. And Sleepy Joe doesn't wear one in his basement either.

"One more thing, why is it that every time you talk, Melania, you remind me of Green Acres and Eddie Albert?"

"Ti si prifuknjen!"

"What the hell does that mean?"

"Literal translation from Slovene: "You are fucked up!" Who is zis Eddie Albert? Vas he at a Vite House dinner?"

"Green Acres was a television show from my youth. Eddie Albert played the role of a Midwestern farmer with a Swedish wife, played by Eva Gabor. You sound just like her."

"Eva Gabor? She Hungarian, you butec. Achhhhhhh. Naj te koklja brcne!"

"I guess I probably shouldn't ask what that means. But what does it mean?"

"Slovene curse phrase. Literal translation: "Let the hen kick you!" (I add "You muzzerfucker.")

"One other brilliant move on my part. You know that WWII ceremony with those 95 year olds? I selected those old farts in particular because they were registered Democrats. No way I wear a mask when breathing on Democrats!"

"Seriously, Donald, you must reconsider your position on masks. You must."

"You mean Elon Must or Elon Mask? (President chortles again at his unbounded wit). "Absolutely not. Cloth masks don't work anyway. They block only, maybe, 70% of particles, so they're worthless."

"Donald, Donald, Donald, have you never heard of convexity or antifragility?"

"No, I haven't, but I think I'm about to find out."

"Convexity is a situation vith uncertain outcomes vere ze upside is much greater zan ze downside. Ve should alvays look for convex situations. If ze mask stops ze infection, zat is a big upside. If it does not, zen not vearing a mask vould have yielded ze same result, so no downside to vearing a mask."

"But it is still only 70% effective."

"No, no, no, you butec. Let me first explain about wiruses."

"Stop, Melania, stop. What the hell is a "wirus?"

16

"A wirus! Vat is a wirus? You have been fighting a wirus for three months now (like a piece of shit, by ze vay) and now you ask vat a wirus is? I tell you. A wirus is a submicroscopic infectious agent (submicroscopic, not invisible, you moron) composed of genetic material (long molecules of DNA or RNA; our wirus is RNA), a protein coat called the capsid, and sometimes an outside envelope of lipids (our wirus has one). Ven zis agent is outside of ze cells of a living host, it is called a virion. So actually, SARS-CoV-2 particles lying on surfaces or expelled in a cough or sneeze are virions, not technically wiruses. Once ze virion enters a host cell to replicate, it is zen technically called a wirus. Vith me so far?"

"Sure. Continue." (To himself: "I really wish I had my ball swinging thingy with me now.")

"OK, next. Vone little virion isn't much to vorry about. It's even smaller zan your hands. So it takes a lot of virions to actually infect a person to get zem potentially sick. Ze amount of virions to cause infection is called ze wirus's infectious dose. Scientists don't know yet vat SARS-CoV-2's infectious dose is. Zay sink it is rather low and zat is vone of ze reasons vhy it is so transmissible."

"But what about the damn cloth masks? They only filter out 70% max, so they're worthless. Can we get to the point here?"

"OK. Let's assume zat SARS-CoV-2's infectious dose is 25. Dragutin and Mojca are having close conversation. Neither is vearing mask. Mojca is actually COVID-19 positive and she sneezes, putting 120 virions into Dragutin. He is shit out of luck. But maybe Dragutin is vearing mask vith 70% effectiveness. Zen he gets 36 virions and is still shit out of luck. But, and here is ze point zat many people don't understand, if both Dragutin and Mojca are vearing mask, zen only 11 virions (120*.3*.3) enter Dragutin. Zat is below ze infectious dose and Dragutin can eat all ze kranjska klobasa and prekmurska gibanica he vants, vashed down vith lots of slivovica schnapps, and feel fine (except for ze farts and burps)."

"Wow. I didn't realize you were so smart. But honestly, if I had wanted to marry someone really smart, I would have hit on RBG."

"RBG? Who is RBG?"

"Supreme Court Justice Ruth Bader Guilfoyle."

"Vat? Zere is no Supreme Court Justice Guilfoyle. Zat's ze name of Don Jr.'s girlfriend - ze vone you always call out "Gargoyle" moaning in your sleep. Supreme Court Justice is zat nice lady Ginsburg."

"Oh yeah. The totally inconsiderate one who won't resign or die so I can nominate David Duke to the Court. Changing the subject, who came up with this convexity and antifragility thing you mentioned?"

"It comes from a very smart mathematician and trader named Nassim Taleb - vone of ze vorld's foremost experts in probability theory and especially in fat tailed risks."

"Uh. Well, if you want some advice about fat tailed risks, I would suggest laying off the twinkies for a while."

(Melania storms out of the room, muttering something in Slovene that is best left untranslated.)

Right on Cue - #2

"Send the Vice President in. And send him in now. And send him in right away. That means I want to see him now. You know, now."

(A few minutes later, Vice President Pence, immaculately dressed and coiffed enters the Oval Office and sits down in front of the President, who is seated at the Resolute Desk. The President hurriedly puts away his favorite ball swinging thingy, hoping Pence did not notice.)

"That's OK, Mr. President. No need to hurriedly put away your favorite ball swinging thingy. Everyone in the West Wing knows how fond you are of it. But did you hear that the latest scientific research on the coronavirus strongly suggests that the virus loves to settle down on shiny, metal round-shaped thingies and can stay there for weeks? Katie Miller had one of those."

(President throws his favorite ball swinging thingy across the room with a fury and recoils in horror.)

"But the research also shows that any coronavirus that has settled on shiny, metal round-shaped thingies is exquisitely sensitive to disinfectants like Lysol and Clorox." (Pence turns to the side, puts his right arm to his face, and barely manages to stifle a huge guffaw.)

"Thank you for the information, Mike. Earlier this afternoon, I was sitting with Melania in the East Wing. She started talking about things I had never even heard about - virions, infectious doses, viral load, convexity and maybe even some other stuff I didn't understand at all. Do you know about any of that stuff?"

"Actually, I do, Mr. President. Because you had the great leadership of appointing me to humbly serve you as Head of the Coronavirus Task Force, I thought that the least I should do was to learn as much of the science as I could, recognizing that I am not a scientist and do not have the special, innate genius for all of this that you have, as you have so masterfully demonstrated."

"Well, anyway, I'm getting a lot of flak from Melania about not wearing a mask. You dealt with this just last Friday in Iowa. And you handled it beautifully. I would like you to tell me the story."

"Of course, Mr. President. But I have already told you the story eight times. Are you sure you want to hear it again?"

"Oh, yes. I simply love that story. Love it. It's beautiful...and lovable...and beautiful... Tell it again."

"As you wish, Mr. President. Last Friday, I was scheduled to participate in a Food Supply Roundtable in Iowa which included executives from five food industry companies (including the infamous minority and immigrant killing champion of all the meat packing companies - Tyson Foods. Better killer than even Mike Tyson). The executives were gathered around the table awaiting my entrance, to be made under your powerful leadership, Mr. President. But there was a problem. All of these butchers were wearing masks - an unpardonable sin. So I sent out a staffer to tell them the masks must be removed. And, as an added bonus, if they did so, I would make sure each of them was included in the next round of $1200 stimulus checks even though they each made $32.6 million a year. They needed no further persuading and gladly tossed aside their masks. And, of course, this was just after my press secretary Katie Miller tested positive for the coronavirus and I often spend time close to her, but never close to her unless there are at least 14 other people around." (Pence shudders.)

(Trump is beaming and bouncing up and down on his chair.)

"I really love that story. And, if you think about it, it is kind of a metaphor (fancy word, eh?) for this whole coronavirus stuff here in America."

"How so, Mr. President?"

"Well, you know that we cannot allow ourselves to wear masks because that would undercut the illusion that everything is ready to go back to normal. And we have the People's Liberate Army in reserve just in case. So you heroically fed the lie and encouraged people to resume normal life by putting five executives at increased risk of dying. So, in a sense, we have shown that people are willing to die to get me re-elected."

"If I might just put a nuance on that noble sentiment, sir. We are willing to let people die to get you (and me) re-elected."

"Same thing. The result is what matters. What did Fauci's great great great great great, really really really great grandfather say? "The end justifies the means." I think the guy's name was Mackaveloni or something, you know, one of those one name guys."

"Absolutely, sir. Will there be anything else?"

"One thing more. I want you to compliment me on my latest fantastic tweet."

"Which one of the 739 weekend tweets was that, Mr. President? They were all so inspiring it's hard to know to which you refer."

"The one that said:

«Game on! We are thrilled to announce the reopening of @ trumpgolfla beginning Saturday May 9th! We look forward to welcoming you back. Book your tee time now!»

"I will gladly compliment you, sir. As you know, people have by now lost count of the number of times you have exhibited unadulterated narcissism, stupidity, tone-deafness, complete lack of empathy, self-absorption, lunacy, incompetence, all made to seem even larger by the smallness of your hands and other parts (so I hear from Melania, but there were at least 14 other people around us in the room when she told me.) But, this one tweet, this one brilliant, inspired, deranged tweet, takes the fucking cake........Oh my god, what did I just say? I need to wash with soap - not my hands, my mouth."

"Mike, you've been a great help today. Go get that soap. And make sure you don't quarantine!"

(Pence leaves the Oval Office visibly shaken.)

Here Come Da Fauch

(Dr. Anthony Fauci arrives in the Oval Office.)

"Good morning, Mr. President. You requested an update on our scientific efforts."

"Yes, I did. Thank you for coming, Tony. Let's start with the vaccines. Where are we on this?"

"Well, sir, this is a very promising area in which we have moved with breathtaking speed. There currently are eight vaccine candidates worldwide that have begun human clinical trials. If I might take the liberty of identifying my particular favorite, it would be the vaccine candidate from Moderna, a company based in Cambridge, Massachusetts."

"Why that one?"

"Well, it uses a new vaccine platform technology called messenger RNA that essentially..." (at this point the President interrupts)

" No, no, no. Stop working on that one. I will not stand for it! I hate that one!"

"If I may be so bold as to ask what your objection is, sir? This vaccine candidate really could save millions of lives."

"It sounds too much like that ugly CDC bitch with the highfalutin sounding name that ruined my trip to India."

"If you mean Dr. Nancy Messonnier, I have to tell you that she is a highly respected professional. She is the Deputy Director,

National Center for Immunization and Respiratory Diseases at the CDC. Surely, sir, you are not suggesting that an imagined similarity between her name and the type of vaccine platform (Nancy Messonnier vs messenger RNA) provides clinical justification for eliminating funding for the Moderna vaccine."

"I sure as hell am. That damn bitch ruined my state visit to India. When I heard what she said, I puked all over Jashodaben Narendrabhai Modi's sari. (Ed. note – She is the wife of Indian Prime Minister Narendra Modi.) Of course, I immediately said "sorry, Jishepoienieoubn." She seemed to get even more angry. And what was even worse, I was so upset on the flight home that I puked again, this time on Melania. Ever since then, she has been referring a lot to her uncle Slobodan, the pig farmer."

"Yes, sir. Perhaps we should move on."

"Good. Update me on therapeutics. I know that "...this is a disease that attacks...health." (Ed. note - Actual quote from the lips of Donald Trump on May 13, 2020.)

"Yes, sir. COVID-19 is indeed a disease that attacks health. Damn, another one of those health-attacking diseases. Just our luck. But therapeutics is an interesting and challenging area, sir. You have probably heard of the anti-viral drug remdesivir. It is not a blockbuster; only provides modest benefit to severely ill patients. But I am cautiously optimistic about convalescent plasma, hyperimmune globulin and the next generation from those, which is synthetic antibody treatment. Shall I describe these very exciting areas to you, sir?"

"No. Sounds rather boring. But I do want to know why this remdesivir isn't more effective. What color is it? "

"It comes in the form of a little blue pill." (Fauci knows full well it is given by intravenous infusion, but he is prone to surrendering to the mischievous little imp inside him.)

"Well there's your problem! Little blue pills don't work. I can tell you from personal experience that little blue pills have no effect. I have taken lots of them - lots and lots and lots of them. Never any response. Not even the slightest hint of any movement. So just change the color and we'll have a blockbuster."

"Excellent analysis, sir. Perhaps I should first consult with Bob Dole? He seemed pleased with it." (Fauci barely suppresses a giant chuckle.)

"Now tell me what you think of hydroxychloroquine."

"It's great if you have lupus. It sucks if you have COVID-19............. What are you doing, sir? You're turning blue!"

(President is seen holding his breath until he is blue in the face. Then lets it out and flails his arms.)

"OK, forget hydroxychloroquine. Which has fared better in clinical trials - Lysol or Clorox?"

"I'm afraid I'm not familiar with any clinical trial involving those potential therapeutic, albeit robustly toxic, agents."

"What? I issued an Executive Order that a clinical trial be held injecting Lysol into one 50 million person cohort and Clorox into a second 50 million person cohort. All on a double blind, non-placebo controlled basis. My buddy Vladimir hacked into the voting registries of every state and provided me with the names of all of the registered democrats. It's from that pool that clinical trial participants were to be recruited."

"Oh, yes. Now I remember. The clinical trial with participants including McConnell, McCarthy, Cornyn, the entire states of Alabama, Mississippi, and Texas, no one from California or Massachusetts. I think the trial is moving right along, sir." (Fauci stifles another big grin.)

"Dammit, Vladimir, you were supposed to find me blue, not red!"

"Shall we move on, sir?"

"I guess so. Testing. Tell me all about our wonderful, beautiful, stupendous, superfluous, unnecessary, vastly overrated testing."

"I don't understand your hostility towards testing, sir. Prior to obtaining a vaccine, it is probably our most powerful tool in fighting the virus."

(The President explains his hostility towards testing. This is an actual quote from his lips on May 14, 2020).

"When you test, you have a case. When you test, you find something is wrong with people. If we didn't do any testing we would have very few cases."

"I'm not sure why that logic has escaped all of us scientists heretofore. Anyway, we are currently doing around 300,000 diagnostic tests per day. Those are the ones that determine if a person is carrying SARS-CoV-2. The standard test is the nasopharyngeal one, where they put the swab down your nostrils until they see daylight. The other diagnostic test is the rapid result test from Abbott. But a recent study by NYU found a 48% false negative rate for that one and the FDA is investigating."

"Isn't that the one we use at the White House?"

"Yes, sir, it is."

"And it might not work?"

"It might not. But you could always wear a mask, sir."

"Absolutely not. In a way, I've been wearing a mask my whole life trying to hide the piece of shit person I really am from the outside world."

"Might I suggest a more effective mask for that one, sir?

"Would you like an update on anything else, sir?"

"Well, what's particularly important in the upcoming weeks?"

"I would say tracing, sir."

"Great. Finally something that I have a lot of experience with and lots of knowledge. Let me show you."

(President opens almost every drawer of the Resolute Desk and resolutely empties their contents onto the surface of the desk.)

"Holy shit, Mr. President. I have never seen such a vast collection of tracings - animals, buildings, golf courses, people, Lysol bottles, hydroxychloroquine pills, autocrats from around the world, Mar a Lago, Hermes scarves (really?). It's truly amazing that you would have kept all your tracing paper drawings from when you were five years old."

"Five years old? No, no, no, Tony. This collection all comes from the time I have been in office. And look at this pile. All of them are from February 2020 - see, I even dated and signed them. This way, when those Do Nothing Democrats and the Fake News people yell and scream that I spent all of February doing nothing, I have the evidence to prove them wrong."

"Uh, right, Mr. President. I actually had a different type of tracing in mind, but it's not important right now."

"Good, because I need to get back to work. What do you suggest I trace next?"

"I'm sure your judgment and expertise on this far exceeds mine, sir."

(Dr. Anthony Fauci leaves the Oval Office.)

A Second Opinion

(Dr. Deborah Birx arrives in the Oval Office.)

"Welcome Deborah. How nice to see you. And I must say that today's scarf is most especially flattering for you. Would it be alright if I fondled it a bit?"

"No problem at all, Mr. President. After all, the President can do whatever the President wishes to do. I am at your service."

"I just got a scientific update from Dr. Fauci, but I would like your perspective on things. First, what do you think of that horrible messenger RNA vaccine named after Dr. Nancy Messonnier, the bitch?"

"I agree with you completely, sir. I never trusted people with long last names. Mine is much easier to write. And the color combinations I've seen on that woman - well, it's enough to give you cephalgia."

"Cephalgia? Is it contagious?"

"Headache, sir."

"Oh. Anything else on vaccines?"

"Nah. If we get one, we get one. Heck, I've been working on an HIV vaccine for years without much success. So if I were you, I'd play down its importance a bit."

"Good idea. And now to therapeutics. You know, that stuff that makes you better."

"Yes, I am familiar with the term, sir. Are you interested in the ones that are designed to combat viruses that attack health?"

"Absolutely. I'm all ears."

"There really are very exciting developments. The Chinese discovered a compound they dubbed 11a that inhibits the protease of the virus, i.e., the enzyme without which the virus cannot survive. Then there is a promising anticancer drug called PB28 which was shown to be 20 times more effective than hydroxychloroquine at deactivating SARS-CoV-2 and might be a lot safer at higher doses. And there is a three drug cocktail of interferon beta 1-b, lopinavir-ritonavir, and ribavirin which has shown promise in treating mild to moderate cases of COVID-19."

"You didn't mention the little blue pill that I discussed with Dr. Fauci. It sure would be great if we could make it a lot more effective. It could then be really big."

"Oh, Mr. President, really. We should move on to the next item."

"Before we do, I'd like to personally thank you for two very important things you've done recently. The first has to do with the time in early April when your 10 month old granddaughter was very sick with a fever of 105. You refused to go and see her and use your formidable medical skills to help her because you feared bringing whatever she had into the White House. Despite everyone saying how heartless and inhuman that was, I salute your devotion to the Supreme Leader. As I said then (Ed. note - this is a direct quote from the lips of Il Duce on April 6, 2020): "But you did not get there? But you did not get there? Good, I'm happy about that."

"And the second thing, Mr. President?"

"Oh, yeah. I love how you took that old fungus chin Redfield's 68 page guidance for re-opening the economy, compiled by the best minds at the CDC at your request, and handed them over to your neighbor's 7 year-old semi-autistic son Oskari (Ed. note - Oskari's parents are from Finland - Sauli and Sanna Vanhanen, nice couple.). The six "decision trees" he produced are exactly what I would have come up with if I had been able to turn off Fox News. But this exercise should teach you an important lesson in life, Deborah."

"And what might that be, Mr. President?"

"Never ask a question you might not like the answer to. That's why, whenever I want some data or information or whatever, I always tell the experts first what I want to hear from them. So much easier that way."

"Anything else today, sir?"

"You know what, I'm getting kind of tired of all this scientific stuff. We can finish up another time. I'd like to get back to my tracing work."

"Excellent idea, Mr. President. Governors all over the country are working on the very same thing. And I think some of them are sharing what they have come up with."

"Wow. Looks like I started a trend. I'm sure many of their tracings are pretty good, but I am even more sure that mine are the best, the most beautiful, the most faithful to the underlying picture, the ones with the fewest smudges."

(Dr. Birx leaves the Oval Office with a perplexed look on her face, muttering "Smudges?")

Origins

(National Security Advisor Robert O'Brien arrives at the Oval Office.)

"Come in, Bob. Sit down. You said it was urgent."

"Yes, Mr. President, I'm afraid it is."

"OK, go ahead. You have three minutes. Then Fox & Friends is on."

"Well, sir, do you recall the top secret biological weapons research you approved regarding the use of novel coronaviruses to spread disease?"

"Umm...Refresh my memory. When would I have done that?"

"Four days ago, sir."

"Ah, yes. Now I remember. That was a really good research idea I approved - a way to encourage reading by linking it with drinking Mexican beer. I remember checking with Secretary DeVos. She was all in favor as long as public schools were excluded. How's the research going?"

" Good and not good, sir. We were able to develop such a virus and learn a lot about it in warp speed."

"So what's not to like? Hurry, you have 52 seconds."

"The virus escaped its containment and infected two research assistants. It could trigger a pandemic."

"OK, Bob. Can you come back around 2:00 pm?"

"See you then, sir."

(National Security Adviser Robert O'Brien returns to the Oval Office promptly at 2:00 pm.)

"Come in, Bob. We were talking about beer?"

"Not quite, Mr. President. Two of our research assistants in a top secret virology lab are infected with a novel coronavirus. This virus has the potential to kill a lot of people and it's right here in the U.S."

"Do we know anything else about it?"

"Only that people with Type O blood have a better chance of surviving an infection."

"Thank you, Bob. I'll let you know when we come up with a plan."

(An urgent meeting is arranged for that evening in the Oval Office. Only the President's most trusted confidantes are invited - Ivanka Trump, Jared Kushner, Donald Trump, Jr., and NSC staffer Hu Mi Tel.)

(When all are gathered, the President explains the situation.)

(Don, Jr.) "Well, we have to get rid of those two research assistants. I say shoot them."

(Jared) "No, that's too medieval. We need to go high tech. I can get some of my Silicon Valley buds to create a super high tech neutrino powered nanoparticle force field of gamma beta wavelength."

(Don, Jr.) "And what the fuck will that do?"

(Jared) "Not sure. It will either act as a containment field around the two research assistants or will generate a black hole that will suck up the entire East Coast. Or, then again, it most likely will do nothing."

"Ivanka, any ideas?"

"Yes, actually I do. We send the two research assistants to the Wuhan Virology Lab without telling the Chinese about the virus. It will start spreading there and we can blame the Chinese for unleashing this virus on the world."

"Now that's my girl! Let's do it!"

(One month later. The novel coronavirus has been declared a pandemic and is inexorably making its way back to the US. The President is in a panic. He calls for Physician to the President Dr. Sean Conley.)

"Sean. Is this beer virus coming here?"

"Almost certainly, sir."

"I mean, is it coming here, in this room? I don't give a shit about New York."

"We canna dismiss the possibility, sir."

"Huh? Could you please put down those damn bagpipes?"

"Aye, sir. I canna disobey an order."

"So, it's possible than I can get infected."

"Aye, sir."

"And if I do?"

"Seeing as you're a bodach gurk (rather stout old man) and given your other health conditions, laddie, I would say it would be a bonnie thing for that pretty lass of a daughter of yours to start making the arrangements."

"But isn't there a certain blood type that can protect a person?"

"Well, we don't know for sure, laddie, but the research does show that people with blood type O have some protection."

"And what blood type am I?"

"Type A, sir."

"Huh. Well, then. Change my blood to Type O."

"Excuse me, sir? What did you say?"

"I said I want one of those blood transfigurations or whatever they call it. It can be done at Walter Reed."

"I believe you are referring to a transfusion, sir. But transfusions must be done with the same blood type or all sorts of unwanted side effects and adverse events can occur. In fact, I think changing a person's blood type has never been done in medical history, at least not successfully."

"I don't care. I want it done. And I want it done now."

Good God, laddie! Yer bum's oot the windae. (You're talking rubbish.)"

"Since you "canna" disobey an order, send the referral over to Walter Reed and tell them to do the other thing at the same time."

"If you insist, sir, but I strongly encourage you to reconsider."

(Dr. Conley leaves the Oval Office shaking his head.)

"Conley!"

"Yes, sir?"

"You forgot your bagpipes."

(One week later in the operating room at Walter Reed National Military Medical Center.)

"Well, the blood change operation is done. Our President now has Type O blood."

"Yes, but who knows what the future side effects might be?"

"I'm afraid we are going to find out. Well, our part is done. Let's call in the plastic surgery team."

(The two plastic surgeons enter the operating room.)

"I've got the specifications for the enlargement right here."

"Wait, I've got specifications for a different body part. What should we do?"

(They scratch their collective heads.)

"Well, both parts show obvious signs of clinical dwarfism. Let's enlarge both."

(The surgery is completed and the President returns to the White House a few days later.)

(One month later, the chief plastic surgeon decides to call Melania for an honest assessment of the results of the two enlargement surgeries.)

"Mrs. Trump, thank you for taking the time to speak with me. So what do you think?"

"As for the hands, vell, he goes around now giving ze finger to everyvone he sees, even to me and to Barron. Seems like zat finger von't relax. I don't really care and Barron, he thinks it's funny. Best of all, our pet parakeet Luka now has another place to wrap his claws around."

"And, um, well, what about the other?"

"Ze other? How should I know?"

"OK. Thank you for your time, Mrs. Trump."

(Surgeon is heard to mutter under his breath - "Maybe that piece I found on the floor was important after all.")

(One month later, Dr. Sean Conley returns to the Oval Office.)

"Sean, some weird things have been happening to me lately. But first, you have to promise to drop that phony Sean Connery wannabe accent. OK?"

"Righty rooney, El Presidente. What's the problem?"

"Lately, I've had some trouble lifting a glass of water to my mouth and keeping it steady. And I have a lot of difficulty walking down a ramp if there are no handrails."

"Hmm.... Does the color of the handrails make a difference?"

"I haven't noticed."

"Have you noticed a difference between tap water and Evian?"

"In taste or lifting?"

"Lifting, of course."

"No difference."

"San Pellegrino? Fiji Water? What about orange juice? Or apple juice? Dragon fruit mango?"

"Same problem with all of them."

"Shit!"

"Shit?"

"Shit."

"Is that a medical term?"

"Aye, I mean yes."

"And it means?"

"It means you're fucked. I was afraid of this. You have developed two rare side effects of the blood type change procedure."

"Is there anything you can do to cure this?"

"I'm afraid not, sir. The conditions are incurable and progressive, meaning they will get worse over time. There is, however, one drug that has shown eency weency evidence of being able to slow the progression, but the data are suspect."

"What's the name of this drug?"

"Hydroxychloroquine."

"Never heard of it, but get me as much as you can and make up some excuse why I'm taking it."

(Dr. Conley leaves the Oval Office.)

"Conley!"

"Yes, sir."

"You forgot your bagpipes again."

Hydroxy and Me

(The scene shifts to the White House briefing room. An unfamiliar figure walks to the podium, facing a gaggle of socially distanced White House correspondents.)

(Ed. note - All questions described here are from actual White House correspondents of major media outlets. Their specific identities are being withheld to protect them from any possibility of retribution by the President squirting them with a water pistol filled with liquid bleach.)

"Good afternoon, everyone. My name is Commander Sean Conley. My official title is Physician to the President. I am the Director of the White House Medical Unit, which is responsible for the medical needs of the President of the United States, the Vice President, White House staff, and visitors. I give these credentials so that, no matter what I might say in response to your questions, you will hopefully keep in mind that I actually do know my shit. I would like to begin with the statement I released yesterday.

"As has been previously reported, two weeks ago one of the President's support staff tested positive for COVID-19. The President is in very good health and has remained symptom-free. He receives regular COVID-19 testing, all negative to date. After numerous discussions he and I had regarding the evidence for and against the use of hydroxychloroquine, we concluded the potential benefit from treatment outweighed the relative risks. In consultation with our inter-agency partners and subject matter experts around the country, I continue to monitor the myriad studies investigating potential COVID-19 therapies, and I anticipate employing the same shared medical decision making based on the evidence at hand in the future.

"Now, I will take your questions."

" Can you tell us, in plain English, what the fuck you just said?"

"Of course. The President wanted to take hydroxychloroquine. I wanted to keep my job. Pretty simple really."

"So the President started taking hydroxychloroquine in response to the two White House staffers who tested positive for COVID-19?"

"Actually, no. That is sort of what I implied and is a logical, but incorrect, assumption. What really happened is that, around that time, the President thought he heard a mosquito whining around the Resolute Desk in the Oval Office. (You know that infuriating sound.). Anyway, the President panicked, screaming that he was going to get malaria. From his research on hydroxychloroquine, he remembered that it is used as a prophylactic against malaria and demanded that we give it to him."

"Has it worked?"

"I am pleased to report that the President shows no signs of malaria except for the facial coloring of a bag of Cheetos. However, that is not a recent phenomenon."

"But aren't you concerned about the potential for adverse cardiac events from taking hydroxychloroquine? Specifically, QT interval prolongation, ventricular tachycardia, and ventricular fibrillation?"

"We evaluated those risks carefully. We were persuaded by a study done in Papua Guinea investigating correlation between heart size and susceptibility to adverse cardiac side effects of hydroxychloroquine. The study found that the smaller the heart size, the smaller the risk of adverse events. As you probably know, the President's heart is so small that you could fit 20 of them in Mitch McConnell's turkey wattle chin."

"Sounds like an impressive study. How many participants were there?"

"We think there were three."

"Was it double-blind placebo controlled?"

"We think all participants could see, despite the fact that they and the lead trial investigator were completely shit-faced from the indigenous alcoholic drink made from palm tree roots."

"You keep saying "you think." Don't you actually know?"

"Not really. The study results are available only in the local language of Tok Pisin."

"I understand that hydroxychloroquine is contraindicated in people with a genetic enzyme disorder such as porphyria or glucose-6-phosphate dehydrogenase (G6PD) deficiency. Has the President been checked for this?"

"Duh..."

"I understand the Federal government procured 29 million doses of hydroxychloroquine. How will they be used?"

"Distribution questions like that are outside my purview. But I can tell you that the 17 million doses set aside for the President are safely stored in the men's locker room in the White House basement."

"Could I ask a personal question, Dr. Conley? After all, we don't know you very well."

"Yes, of course. Go ahead."

"You are from Pennsylvania, right?"

"Correct."

"Then why do you speak with a rather awful, phony Scottish accent?"

"Ah, now you are getting personal, but I will answer your question. When I was a teenager, and continuing on into adulthood, I was just terrible with girls. I was so bad that I even struck out with that roly-poly little bat-faced girl that Paul Simon introduced me to. Out of desperation, I tried this Scottish accent, hoping that when I introduced myself, people would think I said "Sean Connery," rather than "Sean Conley."

"Did it work?"

"I don't know if it worked or not, but I can very happily say that I am married to a wonderful woman named Kristin and we have three beautiful children - two boys and a girl."

"And their names?"

"Angus, Ragnall, and Dioiridh."

"It would appear that the President is doing rather well on hydroxychloroquine. I was going to go so far as to say his cheeks are looking rosy, but I guess it would have be an orange variant of the rose family. Nevertheless, he almost shines. In your medical judgment, might this have anything to do with the hydroxychloroquine?"

"That is an astute observation and one I myself have also made. I have thought about it a lot, consulted with colleagues around the world (including Dr. Oz), and pored through medical textbooks and journals. I have concluded that, for some reason, the President and hydroxychloroquine simply have a mutual affinity for each other. The only way I can explain this is that both President Trump and hydroxychloroquine are completely ineffective against COVID-19 and come with dangerous side effects."

(At this point, a group of official looking men enter the room and seize Commander Conley. The leader of the group, who bears a striking resemblance to Dr. No, announces that the American Medical Association and all state licensing boards are revoking Conley's medical license with immediate effect. Conley leaves, as do the assembled White House correspondents. A loud, shrieking, spine chilling cry is heard coming from the direction of the West Wing.)

Uncle Slobodan

(Melania and the President are sitting in the East Wing. Melania carefully brings up a delicate subject.)

"Donald, it has been too many years since I have seen my dear Uncle Slobodan, the pig farmer from Zagorje ob Savi. I think of him constantly now that you smell the way you do. I want you to arrange for him to come stay with us at the White House for a bit."

"No way!"

"DONALD!!!!!"

"OK, OK, I'll have Chief of Staff Meadows make the arrangements. By the way, does he speak any English?"

"Not a word. But don't worry, my sister Ines can come here and translate for him."

(Ed. note - Ines Knauss is Melania Trump's older sister and lives in New York.)

"No way! Not that good for nothing unemployed sister of yours!"

"DONALD!!!!!"

"Alright dear, just teasing."

(A few weeks later. Dear Uncle Slobodan is sitting in the Oval Office with the President. Next to Uncle Slobodan, wearing a mask, is Ines Knauss.)

"Zdravo, Meester Presseedent. Me lernie dobro angleščina on aeroplaneskiy."

(Uncle Slobodan continues in Slovene and removes something from his bag.)

"Uncle Slobodan say he very pleased to meet you and has special gift for you. Hope you like."

(A beaming President rips off the wrapping paper - decorated with baby pigs - and lets out a shriek of joy.)

"This is fantastic. A brand new, shiny ball swinging thingy with baby pigs hand painted on the balls part of the ball swinging thingy. Ines, how do you say thank you in Slovene?"

"You say Hvala vam."

"Well, then, Havdala swam, Uncle Slobodan."

(Uncle Slobodan looks at Ines with a puzzled look on his face. After Ines says something to Uncle Slobodan, he just smiles at the President and nods his head.)

"Well, Ines, could you ask Uncle Slobodan if I could ask him a few questions? I am curious about life in Slovenia."

"Uncle Slobodan say sure. Fire away."

"Do you get American TV in Slovenia?"

"Uncle Slobodan say da. That mean yes."

"You're so helpful, Ines. How would I ever have heard him say "Da" unless you told me he had said "Da." I know that word because my bosom pal Vladimir spent four hours of his precious time to teach it to me.

"What is the highest rated American TV show in Slovenia? What is Uncle Slobodan's favorite show?" And tell him he doesn't have to say it's my coronavirus task force press conferences."

"Uncle Slobodan say highest rated American TV show in Slovenia is Andrew Cuomo's daily coronavirus press briefings. Love PowerPoint."

(Uncle Slobodan interjects here: "New York Strong!" and raises a fist in the air.)

"OK. What about his personal favorite American TV show? Might it have anything to do with his niece's family members?"

"Uncle Slobodan say his #1 American TV show is Flintstones. Favorite is Barney Rubble. But also like Dino. Uncle Slobodan likes you because he say you smell like Dino."

"Yabba Dabba Doo!"

"Uncle Slobodan say "Yabba Dabba Doo."

"Really, Ines, you're getting on my nerves.

"Let's move on. I've met many great strong leaders - Putin, Xi, Kim, Erdoğan. One of my favorites was Slobodan Milošević. Has Uncle Slobodan ever met him?"

"Uncle Slobodan say Milošević horrible man. Was heartless, self-centered, power hungry, stupid authoritarian who caused great suffering for his people, especially Serbian and Croatian pig farmers. Also, Milošević from Serbia, not Slovenia. If Uncle Slobodan ever see Milošević (died in 2006), he would spit on him for giving pigs bad name."

"Giving pigs bad name?"

"Uncle Slobodan is proud pig farmer. Uncle Slobodan love his pigs. Milošević look like pig with those ridiculous ears (for a human) and give pigs bad name."

"Touchy, isn't he? Ask Uncle Slobodan if there are any interesting Slovenian proverbs?"

"Uncle Slobodan say he tell you three.

1). When you under pressure, you say you "have a bitch jumping into your ass" - "Kuzla mu v rit skače."

2). When you laugh out loud, you say you "smile like a roasted cat" - "Smeji se kot pečen maček."

3). When you puke, you say "call the reindeers" - " Kličemo jelene."

"Now that last one would have come in handy. Any more? These are fun. Please, just one more. One more, please. Just one."

"Uncle Slobodan pick one out just for big author Art of Deal. "Kupil je mačka v žaklju."

"And that means?"

"Literal meaning is "We bought a cat in the sack." Uncle Slobodan say proverb used when person make really totally shitty stupid deal, especially real estate. He surprised you not know that one."

"One last question for Uncle Slobodan. If he could meet just one person in the US, who would it be?"

"Uncle Slobodan say that easiest question yet. All his life, he has wanted to meet Arnold Ziffel. Big fan of Arnold Ziffel."

"WTF? Who the hell is Arnold Ziffel?"

"Uncle Slobodan surprised to hear you say that. Arnold Ziffel, also known as Arnold the Pig, was big TV star of Green Acres. He win three PATSY awards (Golden Globes for non-human actors). Pig farmers in Slovenia all members of Slovenian Ziffel's Society (please not confuse with Slovenian Syphilis Society). But Uncle Slobodan say he know Arnold not alive anymore."

"I think that's all my questions for now. Does Uncle Slobodan have any questions for me?"

"Uncle Slobodan say he have two questions. First question. On pig farm in Zagorje ob Savi, Uncle Slobodan always stepping in shit.

No surprise, then, he is often full of shit. But Uncle Slobodan no see any pigs around White House, so why is President so full of shit? Second question. Dear sweet niece Melanija is intelligent, beautiful, and caring. How the hell did she end up with schmuck like you?"

(With that, the first day of Uncle Slobodan's month long visit comes to an end. He leaves the Oval Office, muttering "Trump je kup sranje."

EPISODE XIII

Intelligence?

(Secretary of State Mike Pompeo enters the Oval Office carrying a small box and a piece of scrap paper.)

"Mike, I'm so happy to see you. Finally, I get to talk to someone who isn't one of those brainy people. What's in the box?"

(Secretary Pompeo opens the box and removes his own ball swinging thingy. He places it on the table and the two of them start swinging, but hopelessly out of sync.)

"Where did you get it, Mike? It's a nice one."

"I'm not really sure, Mr. President. One of my staffers picked it up for me while he was walking my dog, picking up my laundry, and getting Chinese take-out from the Chinese Happy Buddha restaurant on K Street."

"Was it good?"

"The best. They specialize in fortune cookies."

"I'll have to keep that in mind. I hope you brought what I asked for - all of the evidence we've gathered proving that the novel coronavirus was man-made in the Wuhan Institute of Virology."

"I did, indeed, bring everything, sir."

"So where is it?"

"Right here, sir. This small piece of scrap paper. It's all that the massive power of our intelligence services could find."

"Let me see it... I only see two words - "Whew" and "Hon.""

"What is this?"

"Well, our secret listening devices planted in the residence of President Xi picked up this snippet of a conversation he had with his wife while practicing his English."

"Very impressive work, Mike. Now don't lose that piece of paper. And by the way, who in the intelligence community found this?"

"It was the same group that came up with the evidence that Soleimani was planning an imminent attack on 47 American Embassies."

"Well, keep up the good work."

"Will do, sir."

(At this point, Secretary Pompeo has an urgent need to go wee-wee.)

"Would you pardon me, sir?'

"Of course I would. For the personal use of a State Department staffer, for the illegal Saudi arms sale, for the lavish dinners at the State Department designed to solicit potential fundraising for that possible Kansas senate bid, for the taxpayer funded international travel with the wife...But you'll have to be convicted first."

"Uh, I meant that I need to go tinkle really badly. But keep the other thought in mind, if you would."

(Pompeo returns to the Oval Office and lets out a big sigh of relief. Whether that relief is a result of his potty visit or the President's comment is unclear.)

"Oh, by the way, I'm hosting a big party, Mike. Did you get the invitation?"

"You mean the one to the hydroxychloroquine party where you, the Vice President and the entire cabinet sit around drinking beer and popping hydroxychloroquine pills to see who gets the first heart attack?"

"Yeah, that one."

"Wouldn't miss it for the world."

(Secretary Pompeo exits, taking four steps backwards, then bowing.)

A Perfect Call

(A young staffer from the National Security Council wishes to see the President.)

"Come in, son. What is it?"

"Excuse me, Mr. President, but a question has come up at the NSC that only you can clarify."

"Well, I'm used to being the only person that can solve problems, so come in and have a seat. And relax, there's no need to be nervous."

"Yes, sir. I mean no, sir. Or yes, sir. Or no, sir. Ummm...."

"What's your name?"

"Fu On Yu."

"Say that again?"

"Fu On Yu, sir."

"Now, wait just a moment. I said you could relax, not insult me."

"No, sir. I am not insulting you. That is my name - Fu On Yu."

"Well I'll be. I don't remember seeing you earlier today. This is the second shift of the day, right? So you work the second shift?"

"Yes, sir."

"Well then, who has the first shift?"

"Correct, sir."

"What?"

"He has standby duty."

"Who?"

"First shift, sir."

"Who?"

"Right. Who has first shift, sir."

"Why are you asking me? I don't know the NSC staffers."

"I'm not asking you, sir. I'm telling you. Who has the first shift."

"OK. So who has the first shift and what is on standby."

"You're getting it, sir."

"And the name of the person who has night duty?"

"I don't know."

"Is that because you're new to the job?"

"No, sir. We are trained to know everyone's name from the very beginning."

"Then who has night duty?"

"No, sir. I don't know."

"Well, I sure as hell don't either. Remind me, did you tell me why you need to see me?"

"Not yet, sir. And, don't be concerned, I don't mind if you call me by my middle name."

"Huh?"

"In Chinese culture, sir, surname comes first, followed by first given name then second given name. So my name is Fu On Yu, "Yu" being my middle name."

"OK. Let's get to the point, Yu Fu Fu On Yu Yu Fu Yu. or whatever your name is. Why are you here? No. What is it... No. Who sent you? No. Tell me the thing that is needed to tell me. Whew!"

"Certainly, Mr. President. I thought you would never ask. You might recall that you had a phone call yesterday with President Xi of China. A direct transcript of the call was made, but we have lost the audio of the call."

"Yeah, and... What of it? It was a perfect call."

"No doubt it was, sir. However, the respective Presidents on the call are not identified. We cannot determine which speaker is you and which is President Xi. I am here in the hope that you can figure this out."

"I'll certainly try. Should be pretty easy. Do you have the transcript with you? It wasn't a long call."

"I have it right here, sir."

"Then why don't you just read it."

"Yes, sir. Here is the verbatim transcript of yesterday's call with President Xi of China. President Xi's part of the conversation is translated from Mandarin."

"Hello, Mr. President. It is nice to speak with you again."

"Hello, Mr. President. Yes, it is nice to speak with you again."

"I hope you are well."

"Thank you. I am very well and you?"

"Thank you. I also am very well."

"Can we talk about the trade deal?"

"Yes, we can talk about the trade deal."

"I think we need to move quickly."

"I agree. The quicker the better."

"And about the virus."

"Yes, of course about the virus."

"I think it would be good if we both stopped blaming the other for all of our problems. There is plenty of blame to go around."

"Agreed. We stop blaming the other for all of our problems."

"And no more discussion of labs - Wuhan or American military. Right?"

"Right. No more discussion of labs - Wuhan or American military."

"On the important issue of a vaccine. Our vaccine efforts are going quite well. And we have decided that, if we are the first to develop a vaccine, we will share it with the world based solely on who needs it first. What about your vaccine efforts?"

"They are going quite well also. And we have decided that, if we are the first to develop a vaccine, we will first give it to all of our citizens and then sell it to the rest of the world."

"Thank you for a productive call, Mr. President."

"And thank you for a productive call, Mr. President."

(End of call)

"So you see our problem, here, Mr. President. Can you figure out which is you and which is President Xi?"

(The President looks at Fu On Yu Incredulously.)

"We actually pay you a salary? Even a five year-old can figure that one out! It really makes me wonder how they find guys like you to hire. What's your background, young man?"

"I have a Ph.D. in Chinese history, focusing on the leadership succession in the Chinese Communist Party. And I speak fluent Mandarin and Cantonese."

"Huh. Then we have something in common. I also know a lot about Chinese history. And I love fortune cookies. Can't get more Chinese than that!"

"Actually, sir, fortune cookies as we know them have no place in Chinese culture. Our best understanding is that they were introduced into the U.S. by Japanese immigrants. Chinese restaurants in the U.S. seized upon them as a marketing gimmick because desserts were not part of typical Chinese cuisine."

"Show off! Who asked you anyway?"

"He didn't, sir. He knows as much about Chinese culture as I do."

"OK, then, smarty pants. Who was the President of China before President Xi?"

"Correct, sir. Hu."

"No, I'm asking you. I want to know."

"Hu was the previous President of China."

"I told you I don't know! Let me try it a different way. Tell me the latest transition of power in China."

"Hu Xi, sir. Hu Xi."

"How the hell do I know who she is? The next president of China is going to be a woman? Really?"

"I doubt it, sir. Very unlikely. But not impossible. Best woman candidate is Nu Lian-Dong Yu. Then it would be Hu Xi Nu."

"Isn't that always the case."

"We've had a very interesting conversation, sir. Anything else?"

"I would like to know what we're talking about."

"You'd like to know about wat. Certainly."

"Yes, what."

"OK, then. Fortunately, I minored in cultural history of the ancient Khmer kingdoms. The largest religious site in the world is the one at Angkor, referred to as Angkor Wat. It was originally built as a Hindu temple to the god Vishnu in the early 12th Century by the Khmer King Suryavarman II, in present day Angkor. Beginning in the late 12th Century, it was gradually transformed into a Buddhist Temple. One of the first Western visitors to the temple was Antonio da Madalena, a Portuguese friar who visited in 1586 and said that it "is of such extraordinary construction that it is not possible to describe it with a pen, particularly since it is like no other building in the world. It has towers and decoration and all the refinements which the human genius can conceive of." Shall I continue?"

"Not really. I have a headache."

"Well then, I'll call it a night, sir. If you need any further help this evening from the NSC, just pick up the phone and ask for What I Don't Know."

"Me neither."

(Fu On Yu leaves the Oval Office while the President just shakes his head.)

From Russia With Love

(The phone rings on the Resolute Desk in the Oval Office. The President answers it and is informed that Russian President Vladimir Putin is on the line.)

"Hello Vladimir. What a pleasant surprise to hear from you today. Are you going to be using your translator for this call?"

"I think not, Mr. President. As you know, I like to try my English in private conversations like this one, but not so in public situations. Would that be alright with you? Please let me know if I use English words that are too difficult for you."

"Sounds good to me. What's up?"

"I call mainly to thank you for recent help with ventilators that you send us. First 50 ventilators arrive in Moskova today and we look forward to remaining 150 arriving soon. And, that U.S. tax-payers pay for it, is most kind. Please thank American taxpayers on behalf of Rossian people."

"You're quite welcome, Vladimir. Glad to return the favor. After all, you did send us those Aventa-M model Russian made ventilators in April. Just one thing, though. The Fake News media here reported two deadly hospital fires in Russia killing several COVID-19 patients that were traced to problems with that model of ventilator. Is that true and, if so, why did you send us those?"

"Ah, Donald, of all people, I thought you would understand. It is true. But you have problem with high number of coronavirus deaths in U.S., no?"

"We sure do."

"Well, COVID-19 people on ventilators will probably die and add to death count, no?"

"Sure will."

"Best approach is to switch those people to Rossian made model ventilators and have COVID-19 ward catch on fire, killing people on ventilators. Then cause of death is fire, not COVID-19. Numbers stay down."

"Wow. Why didn't I think of that? Any other clever ideas?"

"Da. I mean yes. Actually, you were the ones who first came up with this idea I will mention, but then you really screwed up. I hope you do not mind my saying this, Donald. You are dear friend. I often refer to you as Donald Fredovich Trump – a sign of great comradeship."

"I would welcome some constructive criticism, at least if it comes from you, Vladimir Vladimirovich Putin, who I so greatly esteem. So tell me."

"Your CDC started out with COVID-19 tests that did not work. Always show up negative. If you had stayed with those tests, then even very sick people who later die would test negative and numbers stay very low."

"Huh. How about that? We had the solution to the death count staring us in the face and we didn't see it. Is that why you were so insistent on purchasing millions of those particular CDC tests?"

"Da."

"Getting back to those fire hazard ventilators, do you have any more of those you could send us?"

"I would love to, but I might have big problem here coming up."

"What's that? Anything I can help with?"

"You see, Donald, Rossian winter is very cold. It is so cold that when cattle pee, they have to keep moving so that the icicles they make don't freeze them to the ground."

"Now that's cold AF. And...?"

"Is very strong Rossian cultural tradition to wear fur coats or hats or collars in winter - especially for women, but also men, including fur-lined jockstraps. Most popular fur is mink. But disturbing news out of Netherlands about mink and coronavirus. Minks on mink farms in Netherlands tested positive for coronavirus and transmitted virus to farmers."

"So that's a problem for the Russian city of Minks?"

"Huh? What? Oh, no, you mean city of Minsk. That is capital of Belarus. Lukashenko's problem, not mine. My problem is that when winter comes, and everyone in Rossia is wearing mink coat and hat and collar, I might have really major COVID-19 problem. I do not know what to do."

"I see. But wait, I think I have a solution. Spend the next few months, before winter, gathering all mink apparel in the country and wash everything in very strong bleach. Bleach kills the virus, you know. And close the borders to all new mink that wants to enter the country."

"Interesting idea, Donald. But still problem. If I bleach everything, then I get safety but also get really pissed off population because bleached mink does not look nor feel like real mink. So there is trade-off between allowing people a normal life, on one hand, and safety on other hand. What would you do?"

"Well, I have faced a similar problem here in the U.S., although not with mink. My choice has clearly been to encourage normal life and let safety be damned. I would recommend that course of action to you as well. And you could always make sure every ventilator in Russian hospitals is that fire hazard Aventa-M model."

"Great idea, Donald. Spasiba. And as way of showing my gratitude, I will ask my state hackers to do extra horosho job in 2020 election.

"Dasvidaniya, Mr. President."

"Does with onion to you too, Mr. President."

There Go Da Fauch

(The President asks his secretary to send Dr. Anthony Fauci into the Oval Office.)

(Educational interlude: Dr. Anthony Fauci, born 1940 in Brooklyn, NY, is the Director of the National Institute of Allergy and Infectious Diseases at the National Institutes of Health. He has held that position since 1984, first appointed by Ronald Reagan. He is revered by colleagues around the world as one of the leading experts in immunology and epidemiology. He has been awarded the Presidential Medal of Freedom (George W. Bush), the National Medal of Science and the Mary Woodward Lasker Award for Public Service. In 2019 he was among the inaugural class inducted into the Government Hall of Fame. He has been awarded 45 honorary doctoral degrees from universities around the world. He likes to be called Tony.)

"Yes, Mr. President, you asked to see me. Do you wish to continue our discussion of a few days ago? There is an interesting development about surveillance testing in Seattle."

"No, no discussions. I know you don't think much of me, but here's something I'm darn good at: "You're fired." Clear enough?"

"Very clear, sir. But, as a Federal employee of the NIH, I cannot be fired other than for cause. What reasons do you have to show cause, sir?"

"Rudy predicted you'd say that, so I made a list - wrote it out in my own hand and signed it just so everyone would know it came directly from me."

"May I see it, Mr. President?"

(President hands the paper to Dr. Fauci, on which the President has written, in his own hand, all of his reasons for firing Dr. Fauci.)

"May I read them aloud, sir?"

(Trump nods yes.)

"1). Ivancka is smiten with you and is ignoring Jared.

2). Your poppularity ratings are way higher than mine.

3). Your trustworthness ratings are way higher than mine.

4). You didn't show enough apreciation for my incredible tracing collection.

5). You contradict me all the time.

6). I should have won that Noble Prize. Now you might get it instead of me.

7). You get Brad Pitt to portray you on TV; I'm stuk with that loser Alec Baldwin."

"I'd say that provides ample legal grounds for your dismissal. And that's final."

"Well, sir, honestly this does not come as much of a surprise. And unlike one of the people in this room, I do some forward thinking and planning."

"What does that mean?"

"It means, sir, that I have already lined up how I will continue to devote all of my efforts to serving the people of the United States and guiding them, to the best of my ability, through this nightmare we face. I have arranged to have a 20 minute spot on CNN Monday evening through Thursday evening, alternating between Anderson Cooper and Chris Cuomo. Every Friday evening on CNN, I will host a news conference in which White House correspondents can ask questions. For the weekends, Michael Bloomberg has kindly offered to underwrite a one hour weekly coronavirus update special that all of the major networks have agreed to pick up. And I will be presenting all of this without any scowling faces breathing down my back. Good day, sir."

(Dr. Fauci leaves the Oval Office and is seen kicking up his heels. The President's gaping mouth and bug-eyed stare seem painted on.)

The Long Tentacles of Q

(Donald Trump's personal attorney, Rudy Giuliani, enters the Oval Office.)

"Good morning, Mr. President. You asked to see me."

"I did, I did. I'm feeling very stressed out."

"How can I help, sir? Remember that, because we enjoy attorney/client privilege, you can confide anything to me, no matter how despicable or illegal - just as you have many times in the past."

"No, it's something else this time. I couldn't sleep at all last night because of it."

"Worried about the number of coronavirus deaths?"

"Nah."

"Worried about the massive unemployment figures?"

"That's not it."

"Worried about protests in the streets?"

"Really? Where?"

"Worried about potential side effects from hydroxychloroquine?"

"Nope."

"Worried that Dr. Birx will have to start wearing the same scarf more than once?"

"Shit, Rudy, I hadn't thought of that. Now you've given me something else to worry about."

"Sorry. Worried about how to pronounce the name of Tedros Adhanom Ghebreyesus, the Director-General of the WHO?"

"Rudy, you're not even close."

"Well then, what is it, sir, that is causing you so much distress, so much anguish, so many sleepless nights? You can tell me."

"Isn't it obvious? Can't you see? Look around you, man."

"I know I'm being an obtuse idiot, sir, but I don't understand what you are talking about."

(The President points to the ball swinging thingy on the Resolute Desk.)

"MY BALL SWINGING THINGY IS BROKEN! And, despite staying up all night, I don't know how to fix it. You're my fixer, so FIX IT!"

"First, sir, my condolences on this calamitous event. I will get right on the project of fixing it, even though it is a little bit outside my usual purview. Perhaps I can check with Secretary Pompeo. He has one of these contraptions - a very nice one, too. And if the two of us can't figure it out, we'll go the backdoor channel approach."

"The backdoor channel?"

"Yes, it is well known that the best ball swinging thingy mechanics hang out outside the back door to grab a smoke."

"Do what you can, Rudy. This is really important."

"I'm all over it, sir. But there is something else that concerns me here."

"And that is?"

"How did this happen? And why? And why at this particular point in time? And why is it only the middle ball that seems to be malfunctioning? I'm afraid, sir, that all evidence points to a Deep State conspiracy at work."

"Any ideas?"

"Yes, the overall picture is crystallizing in my mind right now. Shall I explain where I am going with this?"

"By all means."

"As you know, Mr. President, prior to your election, there was a world-wide cabal of Satan-worshipping pedophiles who ruled the world. They funded their operation by running an international child sex trafficking ring from the basement of the Comet Ping Pong pizzeria right here in D.C. This is sometimes referred to as Pizzagate.

"Rudy, when you say cabal, do you mean that nice resort in Mexico?"

"Not exactly, sir. You're probably thinking of Cabo San Lucas. Not the same thing."

"OK, continue."

"Anyway, your election seriously threatened their plans, especially when you faked collusion with Russia to give Mueller cover for his investigation of the Deep State cabal. Thus far, you have thwarted the coup d'état planned by Barack Obama, Hillary Clinton, and George Soros."

"I used to drive a coup d'état when I was into sports cars."

"Yes, sir, but please let me finish. This is serious."

"OK, sorry."

"As I was saying, the cabal is terrified of the coming Storm – when thousands of cabal members will be arrested and sent to Guantanamo Bay prison. The military will brutally take over the country with you as Supreme Leader. The result will be Salvation and Utopia on earth.

"Fearing this, the cabal got desperate. So they hired the Chinese to develop and release the novel coronavirus on the world as a distraction for their attempt to contaminate all ball swinging thingies with mind control force fields by way of quantum tunneling via Ukraine and Turkmenistan."

(Rudy pauses to catch his breath and control his wildly flailing arms.)

"I didn't realize it was this serious. What do you suggest I do?"

"I recommend an immediate travel ban on all metal objects originating in Ukraine and Turkmenistan."

"Well, I know how to deal with Ukraine, but what if the president of Turkmenistan makes a fuss? What's his name, anyway?"

"His name is Gurbanguly Berdimuhamedow."

"Rudy, now you've really flipped out."

"No, that's his name. We can ask him to do us a favor. He opens a bank account in Ashgabat in the name of Hunter Biden with $1 million that we provide and then, at the right time, he announces an investigation. Then we lift the travel ban."

"Sounds like a plan. Get it done."

(Giuliani exits the Oval Office licking his lips in anticipation.)

Das Letter

(The administrative assistant for the Oval Office enters.)

"Good morning, Mr. President. I have your daily security briefing here. Where should I put it?"

"Good God, woman, how many times must I tell you I don't want that thing? I don't read it. I don't look at it. I don't even use it to swat mosquitoes with. And even if I did read it, does anyone actually believe I would understand anything in it? Take it away."

"Good God, Mr. President, how many times must I tell you that I am required by law to personally hand it to you every morning? I don't give a shit what you do with it, when you do it, why you do it, where you do it, or how you do it. Here it is. And one more thing. You got a letter from Germany. The letter is sealed, but the postmark says Kallstadt. Here."

(The administrative assistant exits, leaving the President cowering under his desk.)

(The President tosses the daily security briefing in the trash can and curiously picks up the curious letter.)

"Kallstadt, Kallstadt. Rings a bell, but I don't know why."

(The President turns the letter over a few times and finally opens the envelope and begins to read the contents.)

"Mein lieber Herr Präsident. Wie geht es Ihnen heute........."

(President checks the trash can to make sure he really did throw away the right unintelligible document.)

"Hmmmm. This entire letter is in a foreign language. Let me think. Slovene? Tagalog? Finnish? No, no, no. Wait. It's signed by Angela Merkel so it must be German. But how do I find out its contents in a safe and secure manner without bringing in anyone who maybe should not see it?"

(The President resolutely picks up the red phone on the Resolute Desk.)

"Privyet, Donald. So good to hear from you. What up is?"

"Thanks for taking the call, Vladimir. I have a little problem. I just received a letter - not a very long one - from Angela Merkel. It's written in German and I need a translator I can trust. You speak German, don't you? You know, I'm a little concerned about a letter from Merkel after having received such beautiful letters from my pal Kim Jong Un. Can you help me?"

"Naturlich, Ich spreche sehr gut Deutsch. Ich helfe gern. Sure. Let's do it."

"OK. I'll read a few sentences and then you can translate."

(The President starts to read and then Putin translates.)

"My dear Mr. President. How are you today? I first wish to express my apologies, but I will be unable to attend the G7 conference you were hoping to host at the White House later this month. I have been in close consultation with my health advisers and they are of the opinion that a visit to a coronavirus response challenged nation such as yours would bring unacceptable public health risks to Deutschland upon my return. My advisors were not persuaded about the risk mitigation stemming from your gracious offer to provide all G7 heads of state with a two-week supply of hydroxychloroquine. So, vielen dank, aber nein. Thanks, but no thanks."

"Ungrateful ungrate. Just who does she think she is? I'm actually kind of glad I won't have to listen to her lecturing me all the time. But it is supposed to be a G7, not a G6. I've got an idea. Vladimir, why don't you come to the conference in place of Merkel?"

"Donald, you know I like nothing more than to spend time with Ivanka, but I am sorry. I must turn down gracious offer. Rossia was full member of G8 until 2014. Then Rossia was kicked out of G8 because of little, meaningless, non-event when we invaded sovereign country and annexed Crimea. Was no big deal, but Obama and friends overreact. So, like Angela, must say "Spasiba, but nyet spasiba." Thanks, but no thanks."

(Putin translates.)

"Now to the main purpose of this letter. I am visiting the small town of Kallstadt in the Rhineland-Palatinate state in Deutschland, only 16 miles from Mannheim."

"Vladimir, why would I care what dinky little sewage infested town she's in? I'll continue."

(Putin translates.)

"As you are surely aware - but given your level of general knowledge, maybe not - Kallstadt is the ancestral home of the Trump family. Your grandfather was born here. I am writing this letter while enjoying a delicious Schwarzwälder Kirschtorte (black forest cake) in a wonderful little bakery called the Bäckerei Trump."

"This is getting better, but I still have no idea what's in that woman's head. I'll read on."

(Putin translates.)

"You are maybe wondering why I mention these things. It is to illustrate that here in Deutschland we have successfully dealt with the novel coronavirus and are robustly and safely re-opening our economy. Kallstadt is a great example. Our German experience, along with China, Taiwan, South Korea, Thailand, Australia and New Zealand shows that it can be done."

"Yeah, rub it in bitch, rub it in."

(Putin apologizes for speaking out of turn.)

"I'll continue reading."

(Putin translates.)

"In the United States, of course, your response is reminiscent of a dyslexic ratfuck. Your testing has worked like a submarine with screen doors. Your tracing has all the precision of a finely-tuned German watch with a dead battery, and your quarantines have no Bratwurst or Beck's Bier."

(Putin interjects again.) "No bratwurst or Beck's? Donald, are you insane? Have you no sense of decency?"

(President continues reading and Putin translates, trying his best to control himself.)

(Merkel's letter continues.)

"No wonder the joke that is going viral in Deutschland is: "What borders on stupidity? - Canada and Mexico." Now, Donaldchen, let me get to the point. I have long felt a great affinity for the American people. I care about them dearly. They have been suffering grievously. And that suffering has now been compounded by the coronavirus pandemic. It is just too much. It is my duty to step in."

"Will that Fruitlein ever get to the point? Let's finish this Vladimir."

"I recently announced my intention to step down as Bundeskanzler (Chancellor of the German Republic) in 2021. But I have decided to accelerate that timetable and immediately turn over my duties here so that I might come to the United States and take over all responsibilities of the office you now hold. I will continue such efforts until the coronavirus situation in the United States has reached a par with what we have accomplished in Deutschland and cannot be fucked up again even by you. In case you are worried about your personal future and that of your immediate family, I am prepared to make the following appointments:

Donald Trump - Secretary of Misstate

Ivanka Trump - Head of the Anti-social Security Administration

Donald Trump, Jr. - Secretary of the Put It In My Treasury

Jared Kushner - Non-science Advisor, also known as Nonsense Advisor

Mike Pence - Ambassador to the International Fellowship of Humanists"

(President finishes reading and Putin finishes translating.)

"Donald, I hope you will accept this offer in the spirit of friendship and duty in which it is offered. Mit freundlichen Grüßen, Angela."

(Some activity is heard from the Russian end of the line. The President can make out some words: "Moskova TV 1, 8:00pm, tonight)

"Dasvidaniya, Mr. President, gotta go and get ready for my special broadcast tonight."

"Does with onion to you, too, Mr. President."

Amazing Quark

(The President and Melania are in the East Wing. It looks like they are having a fight.)

"Would you stop that already, Melania? You keep saying the same word over and over and over again - "Quark." This has been going on for three days now. You're driving me nuts. Stop!"

"Donald, I no stop until I get my qvark. Ven I get qvark? Ver I get qvark? Vhy I don't get qvark? You get me qvark, you get me quiet."

"OK, I understand. But why do you need this quark anyway?"

"I vant to make homemade prekmurska gibanica. Vonderful pastry from old country. But cannot make vizout qvark."

"OK, I'll get on it right away."

(The President goes to the Oval Office and asks Kellyanne Conway to come by.)

"Kellyanne, I have a major problem with Melania. She has been screaming for three days that she wants something called quark. She won't stop until I get it for her, but I don't have the slightest idea what it is. You need to help me."

"Certainly, sir, this is something we can work on together. Maybe it has something to do with international affairs. After all, Melania is from Slovenia."

"Good idea. Let's call in Pompeo."

(Secretary of State Mike Pompeo enters the Oval Office.)

"Thanks for coming by, Mike. I've got a problem that I hope you can help me with."

"Sure, Mr. President, whatever I can do."

"Melania is insistent on getting something called quark and I don't know what it is. In her state, I don't dare to ask her. Any ideas?"

"Quark...quark...quark...Let me think...Yes, maybe I've got something. Quark is the second largest city in Ireland, just behind the quapital city of Dublin. It's located in the southwest of Ireland in a quounty of the same name - Quounty Quork in Gaellic. City's population is around 200,000 and it's close to Blarney Castle where the Blarney Stone rests. Problem solved."

"I'm not so sure about that, Mike. I can't imagine why Melania would be interested in a trip to Ireland at this time, but thanks anyway. And how are those speech classes going? Sounds like you've skipped a few."

(Kellyanne has an idea.)

"Drawing upon my political expertise, sir, I think I might have the answer. Perhaps Melania is referring to former Tennessee senator and pain-in-your-ass Bob Quorker. You know, the guy you were considering for Secretary of State at one time."

"But why would Melania be interested in him?"

"Why not? He's kind of debonair and seems like Melania's type - strong, self-effacing, articulate, gentlemanly."

"Kellyanne, if you want to keep that position of Counselor to the President, you're going to have to do better than that. We've got to keep looking."

"Perhaps it's a scientific term. Shall I call in the White House Science Advisor?"

"Yes, let's do that. By the way, what's his name?"

"Kelvin Droegemeier."

"Oh boy, this will be fun."

(The White House Science Advisor, Kelvin Droegemeier, enters the Oval Office.)

"Kelvin Droegemeier, sir. It's an honor to meet you. I believe this is the first time."

"Yes, I'm sure it's an honor to meet me. Sit down, please."

(The President explains the problem.)

"Do you have any ideas?"

"Actually, sir, I have two ideas that I hope will help you with this problem. First, there have been reports of an extraterrestrial, warp-capable humanoid species called the Ferengi. These reports come from a television series in 1987 called Star Trek - The Next Generation. The Ferengi hail from the planet Ferenginar. Their civilization is built on free enterprise, where earning profit is the sole meaningful goal in life, superseding all other endeavors. One of their leading merchants goes by the name of Quark."

"Very interesting. Sounds like my kind of people. Can we invite some of them to the White House?"

"I'm afraid that would be difficult, sir. No one has ever seen a Ferengi other than on TV. There are, however, some conspiracy theories that believe a Ferengi chieftain has infiltrated the White House and enjoys sitting at the Resolute Desk playing with one of those ball swinging thingies."

"OK, so that idea isn't going to work. You said you had another?"

"Yes, sir. Current theory in particle physics holds that a type of elementary particle, with a fractional electric charge, called a quark forms the building blocks of hadrons, such as protons and neutrons. Quarks come in six flavors - up, down, strange, charm, bottom, and top - and three colors - red, blue, and green. They were demonstrated to exist in a series of experiments led by Nobel Prize winner Murray

Gell-Mann (died 2019) at the Stanford Linear Accelerator Center in 1968."

"And where is this Stanford Linear Accelerator Center, as you call it?"

"Why, I believe it's in Stanford, sir. Sort of like the old Grant's Tomb joke."

"Yeah, well, whatever, but what kind of crap science are you peddling? Do you really expect me to believe there's a particle that goes around calling itself a charm quark or a strange quark? Why not a Pelosi quark? Or what would happen if a Chinese president quark merged with a super smart whiz kid quark? Would we get a Xi-whiz quark? No, I don't buy into any of this Fake Science unless you can actually show me a quark. Can you?"

I'm afraid not, sir. Quarks are very, very small."

"How small are they?"

"They're so small that if you placed one quark next to one of your hands, it would require a magnifying glass to determine which was smaller."

"Kellyanne, what's so funny?"

"Nothing, sir, I was still thinking about the Xi-whiz quark."

"Well, Mr... What did you say your name was?"

"Droegemeier. Kelvin Droegemeier, Mr. President."

"Well, Mr. Drugstore, you seem to be pretty darn smart, but I think Kellyanne and I will have to look outside of science for the answer to our problem. You can go now."

(Kelvin Droegemeier leaves the Oval Office.)

"Kellyanne, we seem to be getting nowhere. I need more ideas from you."

"Yes, well, this word "quark" is certainly odd sounding. Perhaps a Professor of English Literature with a high degree of erudition can shed some light on this. Shall I try to get someone on the phone?" (The President nods in the affirmative.)

"Dr. Matthew Bevis, Professor of English Literature at Keble College, the University of Oxford, speaking. To whom do I have the pleasure of speaking?"

"This is Donald Trump, President of the United States of America."

"The honor is all mine, sir. How may I help you?"

"I have Kellyanne Conway with me and we are trying to figure out what is meant by the word "quark." We were hoping that someone of your erudition would be able to help us."

"Someone of my what, sir?"

"Erduition. You know, someone who knows a lot of stuff."

"Ah, yes, now I understand. For a moment there I thought you had a bad mispronunciation of the last name of the president of Turkey. But I think I can help you with your conundrum."

"Great. But could you address my problem first?"

"Of course. There are two possible references in English literature that could be relevant here. The first is from the famous Irish author James Joyce, considered to be one of the greatest and most influential writers of the 20th Century. Surely you have read "Dubliners." No? Then how about "A Portrait of the Artist as a Young Man"? Well then, the famous novel "Ulysses?"

"Stop there. That sounds familiar. I think I watched part of a documentary on him on cable a while ago. Great general. Strong. Powerful. Could really dominate a battlespace."

"Yes, well, moving right along. James Joyce published a novel called Finnegan's Wake in 1939. It was most assuredly avant garde and still is considered to be one of the most difficult novels to read. On page 383 there is the famous line "Three Quarks for Muster Mark!" It is this line that inspired the physicist Murray Gell-Mann to name certain elementary particles "quarks."

"I doubt that's our answer. Melania is not a native English speaker. You mentioned a second possibility?"

"Of course. All English literature traces some roots to the greatest playwright of them all - William Shakespeare. Surely, you have read some of his plays. Hamlet - "To be or not to be, that is the question." No? How about Macbeth - "It is a tale told by an idiot, full of sound and fury, signifying nothing." Would this describe your coronavirus task force press conferences? Uh uh? Then certainly King Lear for someone like yourself . I think you'll like this one - "I am a man more sinned against than sinning" or "Blow winds and crack your cheeks! Rage, blow, You cataracts and hurricanoes." Really strong, really powerful, really dominating, huh?"

"Professor (Kellyanne interjects), can we get back to quark, please?"

"Yes, sorry, I could recite Shakespeare for longer than it takes the President to do 1456 tweets. One of the Bard's most famous plays is Richard III. In Act V, the crippled and villainous King Richard is thrown from his horse on the battlefield and cries out: "A horse, a horse, my kingdom for a horse." That being one of the most famous lines in English literature, there is, nevertheless, some current scholarship questioning its accuracy. Several years ago, a manuscript dating from Shakespeare's time and apparently in Shakespeare's own hand was discovered underneath several cow patties in a pasture near Stratford-upon-Avon. The manuscript very clearly shows the word "horse" crossed out and replaced with the word "quark". These scholars, who some label quacks, thus believe that the true most famous line in English literature, or close thereto, is actually: "A quark, a quark, my kingdom for a quark." Despite intense research, even those holding this view have no fucking idea what Shakespeare could have meant."

"So let me get this straight. After all this time, you've got a book no one understands and some piece of paper underneath cow shit whose accuracy is in dispute and whose meaning no one has a fucking clue about. And you really think this is going to help us?"

"Thank you for your time, Professor."

(Kellyanne ends the conversation.)

"I'm getting rather discouraged, Kellyanne. Is there anything left to try?"

"Well, I'm kind of thinking that "quark" might be some sort of animal sound. Maybe the Director of the National Zoo could shed some light on this. Shall I get him on the phone?"

"Let's try."

"Hello. Steven Monfort speaking."

"Hello Steven. This is Kellyanne Conway. I'm with the President and we were hoping you might be able to help us."

"I'll sure try. But first, Kellyanne, about last Tuesday night at the bar..."

"Later Steven. Later."

(The President explains the problem.)

"This is actually pretty easy, I think, sir. I've got three great ideas. First, "quark" is the sound made by a mythical creature called a dog-duck."

"A dog-duck?"

"Yes, a dog-duck. Ancient Medieval archives uncovered in an Italian monastery dating from the 11th Century describe a chimerical creature that was part dog, part duck. It was called a dog-duck.

A chimera is an organism that has more than one genotype. We all know how hot-blooded Italians can be. Apparently, according to these ancient manuscripts, one particular dog in a small village got so excited he forced himself upon a duck. The resulting offspring was this chimeric dog-duck. At first, the dog-duck was celebrated as a harbinger of good luck. That changed, however, when, two years later, a novel coronavirus made the leap from the dog-duck to humans and the village was pretty much wiped out."

"Fascinating story, but I don't think Melania was screaming at me to get a dog-duck from the pet store. Continue, please."

"The next two possibilities are related. You know, animals do get sick as well as humans. And many of the illnesses are similar. One such illness is pharyngitis, more commonly referred to as sore throat. If a duck - particularly Mallard, Mandarin, Canada Goose, and Donald - get pharyngitis, their quack will sound very much like your word quark.

"Continuing with the illness theme, it is also conceivable that a duck will be inclined to puke. This can be induced by the traditional causes - gastroenteritis (stomach flu), binge drinking, and listening too long to one of your rants. The puking duck will often make a sound very much like your word quark."

"Puking duck, eh? I think I had that for the Chinese take-out dinner last week from the Chinese Happy Buddha restaurant on K Street. Very tasty."

"Perhaps, sir. But also perhaps you are referring to the Chinese delicacy called Peking duck.. In any event, I hope I have been of some assistance."

"Assistance? You give me a dog fucking a duck, a duck taking Cepacol, and a duck running out of barf bags. You call that assistance?

Call ended. Discuss last Tuesday's bar episode with Kellyanne on your own time.

"Whew. I'm really getting discouraged, Kellyanne. We're not getting anywhere on this quark problem."

"Yes, we're both exhausted, Mr. President. Why don't we take a lunch break to clear our heads?"

"Good idea. I'll have lunch brought in. What are you having?"

"Just tell them the usual for me. I have the same lunch almost every day."

(The President orders lunch. Shortly thereafter, the White House butler arrives with two plates which he proceeds to place in front of the President and Kellyanne.)

"What's that white stuff on your plate, Kellyanne? It looks gross."

"Not at all, Mr. President. The White House chef makes the most delicious cottage cheese I've ever tasted. I have it almost every day."

"Excuse me, ma'am. I know it's not my place to speak up here" (says the White House butler), "but that's not cottage cheese."

"It's not? Then what is it?"

"Why, it's a fresh dairy product made by warming soured milk until the desired amount of curdling is met, and then straining it. It is said to have originated in the 14th Century in Eastern Europe."

"Does this delicious dairy product have a name?"

"Yes, ma'am. It's called quark."

(Oh, the look on their faces...)

(Two hours later.)

(Having finally solved the quark mystery and looking forward to some much needed domestic tranquility, the President has a relaxed, contented look on his face when two glum-looking men show up at the entrance to the Oval Office.)

"Well, look who it is - my Attorney General William Barr and my FBI director Christopher Wray. Come in, gentlemen. Why such glum-looking faces? We've solved the quark mystery, or haven't you heard?"

(Bill Barr does the talking.)

"Yes, sir, we heard about two hours ago that you solved the quark mystery. Kellyanne told us of your great success and I can report that Mrs. Trump has all the quark she desires."

"So why the sour faces?"

"You see, Mr. President, there could be a real problem here. Most quark that people use is white in color. But there is also a variety of quark that is black in color. The ratio of white to black quark production is about 80/20. Black quark has the same consistency, taste, and utility in the making of prekmurska gibanica as white quark. But for some reason, many people unfairly consider black quark to be, in some way, inferior to white quark. And all of the quark obtained by Mrs. Trump is white quark."

(Director Wray continues explaining the problem.)

"There is an organization, Mr. President, called the NAACQ - National Association for the Advancement of Colored Quark. In keeping with the domestic surveillance duties of the FBI, we have kept tabs on this organization for several years. Heretofore, all of its activities have been peaceful - usually nothing more than handing out leaflets at the entrance to Whole Foods stores."

(Bill Barr takes up the explanation.)

"But with the recent nationwide protests stemming from increased awareness of, and intolerance for, police brutality and racial injustice..."

(At this point, both Barr and Wray take a knee and remain in that position. Barr continues.)

"...the NAACQ seems to have taken a more strident tone. It has launched a promotional campaign called "Black Quark Matters." We are concerned about the security and public relations issues that could arise if Mrs. Trump discriminates against black quark for her homemade prekmurska gibanica and such discrimination were to become public knowledge."

"So what do you want me to do?"

"It would be best if you could convince your wife not to use only white quark."

(The President unleashes a blood curdling scream, tears at his hair, and mutters: "She'll kill me!")

(Ed. note - Once informed of the situation, Melania Trump decided to go with 50% white quark and 50% black quark in her homemade prekmurska gibanica. It never tasted better.)

Twit-in-Chief

"Get me Jack Dorsey on the line and toot it sweet." (The President barks to his assistant. Ed. note – Jack Dorsey is CEO of Twitter.)

"Good morning. You have reached the corporate offices of Twitter, where, twue to form, we twy to make your day as twuly wonderful as possible."

"Are you guys totally bonkers?"

(The President continues to rant for ten minutes before realizing that he is listening to a recording. Finally, a person comes on the line.)

"Young lady, this is the President of the United States."

"Wow, really? The twit-in-chief! Just a minute, sir, and I will tee up the proper automated prompts."

"If you know your party's extension, you can tweet it at any time. For the misspelled words department, tweet 1. For the bald-faced lie department, tweet 2. For the deranged conspiracy theories department, tweet 3. For tips on how to insult the maximum number of people in 280 characters, tweet 4. For medical advice that is hazardous to your health, including whether non-diabetics should take insulin, tweet 5. For incomprehensible rants, tweet 6. To get the latest on Joe Scarborough, tweet 7. To order or reorder twinkies, tweet 8. To hear this menu repeated, tweet 9."

(The President presses "0"; that usually works.)

"Good morning. You have reached the corporate offices of Twitter, where, twue to form, we twy to make your day as twuly wonderful as possible."

(Twenty minutes later, the President gets to speak to an operator.)

"I demand to speak with Jack Dorsey and you goddamn better do it now."

"There is no reason to raise your voice, sir."

"I'll raise my voice and use whatever goddamn words I want. Do you know who this is? This is the goddamn..."

(The line goes dead and the President is sitting there listening to a dial tone.)

(Jack Dorsey calls the switchboard operator at Twitter.)

"Jennifer, did he call?"

"Yes, sir, he did. Just like you said he would."

"Did you put plan A into operation? Switched him to that special options menu we developed just for him?"

"I did, indeed. Worked like a charm. Then had him on hold for a long time. Then disconnect. I don't think he was very happy, sir."

"Then everything worked perfectly. Next time, you can use the second special options menu, just for a little variety. Keep up the good work, Jennifer."

"Thank you, sir. I'll do my best."

Dorsey vs. Twump

(Jack Dorsey, Twitter CEO, is sitting at his desk with his morning coffee, reading the newspaper. He sees that President Trump signed his threatened Executive Order against social media companies. He calls down to his trusted switchboard operator.)

"Good morning, Mr. Dorsey."

"Good morning, Jennifer. Are you ready for a fun day?"

"Most definitely. Everything is ready to go."

"Great. I'm going to put that Rule Violation notice on the President's Minneapolis tweet right...now. Get ready, because it shouldn't take long."

"Aye, aye, sir."

(Ten minutes later, the phone rings in Twitter's corporate offices.)

"Good morning. You have reached the corporate offices of Twitter, where, twue to form, we twy to make your day as twuly wonderful as possible."

(The President is not fooled this time by the recording and shouts at the recorded voice.)

"You still haven't changed that godawful, looney tune piece of crap recorded greeting. No wonder your company is headed for bankruptcy and I, of all people, should know, shouldn't I? Heh, heh, heh."

"I'm sorry, sir, I didn't quite catch the last part of what you said. Something about looney tunes and bankruptcy perhaps? Would you care to repeat it?"

"Uh, no. No. Thank you. Would you connect me, please, to Jack Dorsey?"

"Certainly, sir. May I tell him who's calling?"

"This is Donald Trump. The frickin President of the United States, so do it now."

"I'll connect you to our dial by name service. Just a moment."

"Hello. This is the Twitter dial by name service. Please enter the last name of the person you wish to reach, followed by the pound sign."

(The President enters D-O-R-S-Y).

"I'm sorry. There is no one at the company by that name. Did you perhaps mean D-O-R-S-E-Y?"

(The President re-enters the name correctly.)

"I'm sorry, that number is not accepting calls at this time. I will forward you to our automated prompts. Please hold."

"Please listen carefully as our menu options have changed. If you know your party's extension, you can tweet it at any time. For a list of the Twitter accounts with the most followers, tweet 1."

(The President defiantly tweets 1, expecting the gratification he has thus far been denied.)

"The fifth most followed Twitter account belongs to Taylor Swift with 86 million followers. In fourth place is Rihanna with 97 million followers. Moving up the ladder, we get Katy Perry in third place with 109 million. In second place is Justin Bieber with 112 million."

"Who the hell are these people? Never heard of them. Damn good thing I didn't lose to these nobodys nobody ever heard of. So, tell me miss Twitter phone voice, how many followers do I have?"

"And the number one Twitter account in the world, with more followers than anyone else, is... Barack Obama, with 118 million followers."

(It's unclear if a face has ever turned that red before.)

"If you wish information on whether all Twitter users are bird brains, tweet 2."

(The President tweets 2 out of curiosity.)

"Whereas it is undeniably true that several notable Twitter users are total bird brains, such mental condition is most certainly not a requirement to have a Twitter account. Indeed, our Twitter bird mascot - Larry the Bird - has a bird's brain but is not a bird brain. And, yes, it is true. Larry the Bird was named after Boston Celtics Hall of Fame basketball legend Larry Bird. One of our co-founders - Biz Stone - grew up in the Boston suburb of Wellesley during the Larry Bird era."

"For the comment of the week that we most wish had been a tweet, tweet 3."

"This ought to be really good - another totally stupid comment by one of those dumb Democrats. Can't wait to hear it."

"On May 27, White House counselor Kellyanne Conway made the following statement: "People are very proud to show up and go to the polls. They really are. I mean, they wait in line for a Georgetown Cupcake for an hour, to get a cupcake. So, I think they can probably wait in line to do something as consequential and critical and constitutionally significant as cast their ballot." Too bad she didn't do this as a pair of tweets. Then we could have fact checked with this notice on Georgetown Cupcake's website: "...effective Tuesday, March 17, all

Georgetown Cupcake locations will only be accepting pre-orders for store pick-up, local delivery, and overnight nationwide shipping. We will no longer be serving customers inside our stores..."

"For information on how to interfere with the 2020 election (which we are not doing), tweet 4."

"Maybe I'll pick up a few ideas."

"We're sorry. We have no information to provide on that subject. We suggest you call 1 (202) 456-1414. When you reach the White House switchboard, ask for the Oval Office. If that is unsuccessful, try to reach Jared Kushner. He knows nothing about the subject, but that never stops him from holding himself out as an expert."

"Jared. Why didn't I think of that?"

"For an assessment of the effects of the latest Presidential Executive Order attacking Section 230 of the Communications Decency Act of 1996 on social media in general and Twitter in particular, tweet 5."

"OK, gotcha now you slimy smarty pants California techie elitists."

(The President tweets 5 with gleeful anticipation.)

(Long silence. Then more silence. A voice finally speaks after three minutes.)

"For those of you slow-on-the-uptake callers still listening, the "nothing" you listened to on the line for three minutes like an idiot is the answer to the question."

"To speak to Jack Dorsey, tweet 6."

(The President tweets 6 with a huge sigh of relief.)

"Hallo. Joey Pisgarian speaking."

"Joey who?"

"Pisgarian. Who 'dis?"

"Who am I???"

"What kinda question is that? Fancy yourself the reincarnation of Jean Paul Sartres? Or maybe you're more into one of the other French existentialist philosophers - Camus or Simone de Beauvoir. Me personally, I take more of a shine to Ionescu, even though he was largely Romanian. So yeah, I'll go along with your metaphysical game of "Who are you?"

"Who am I???"

"Oh, no. Not this again. OK buddy, let me try again. What's your name?"

"My name is Donald Trump and I am the frickin President of the United states!"

"Right buddy, sure."

"No, I'm serious!"

"Yeah, and Ho Chi Minh never died and is doing Elvis impersonations in Vancouver."

"I tell you. I am the President. How can I prove it to you?"

"Let me tink...Got it. Say "I am the greatest." No, wait, that was Ali - twuly the Greatest. Hmm...Say "perspicacious existentialist."

"Perpitackis eggstolentist."

"Alright, I think you are who you say you are. How can I help you?"

"Are you Jack Dorsey's personal assistant?"

"Me? What, are you kidding? I work in sanitation in the basement of Twitter's corporate offices. I deal with shit - big shit, little shit, long shit, fat shit, you get the idea. And, don't tell anyone, but I've got a little business on the side processing shit for Slovenian pig farmers in the Central Valley."

"Well, Joey, can you transfer me to Jack Dorsey?"

"Sure ting. Why didn't you say so at the beginning? And, before I let you go, might I recommend that you take a read through Ionescu's play "Rhinoceros." I'll connect you now."

(The phone in Jack Dorsey's office rings and rings and rings. After ten minutes of waiting, the line goes dead and the President is sitting there listening to a dial tone.)

(30 minutes later, Jennifer (the switchboard operator at Twitter) receives an interoffice memo. "I haven't had this much fun in years. Enjoy your 30% raise. Keep up the good work. Jack.")

Beans, Balls, and Bibles

(The President appears in the Rose Garden for a hastily organized press conference the day following his sojourn to St. John's Church. All questions described here are from actual White House correspondents. Their specific identities are being withheld to protect them from possible retribution from the President unleashing ferocious, but well groomed, French poodles on them.)

"Good afternoon. I'll begin with a short statement. Because I am not reading from notes, it has to be short.

"You all saw what happened yesterday evening when I looked danger in the eye and walked, unguarded, from the White House to St. Jimmy's Church. What you saw was tough. What you saw was strong. What you saw was massive. Did I say powerful?

"End of statement. Now, I will take your questions."

"I believe the name of the church is St. John's Church, Mr. President, not St. Jimmy's. Did you mean St. John's Church?"

"Hell, no. Why would I ever go to a church? My shirt got a little splattered from that pepper spray stuff and I was looking for Jimmy's Cleaners and Alterations in Wallingford, Connecticut and then go for a quick sandwich at a nearby Jimmy John's. Unfortunately, my advance team misunderstood."

"But, Mr. President, you looked very determined as you were walking to the church from the White House. Furthermore, you don't seem like a person who would walk from Washington, DC to Wallingford, Connecticut. Rumor has it that you use one of those self-balancing motorized scooters to go from the salad bar section of the White House lunch buffet to the hot entrees, and you even have the entire dessert table brought to you. So, I hate to say it, but your excuse seems kind of lame."

"How did you find out about Gummy Bear?"

"Gummy Bear, sir?"

"Doesn't everyone give a name to their buffet table self-balancing motorized scooter?"

"Of course, sir. But what was your real motive?"

"Real motive? OK. If I don't get around the buffet table fast, there will be nothing left if fatsos Pompeo and Barr get there first."

"Understandable, sir, but what I meant was what was your real motive in walking to St. John's Church?"

"OK, I'll spill the beans. The previous night, during the protests, someone infiltrated the White House and took something from the Oval Office. As a matter of national security, it had to be recovered. Our intelligence pointed to it being kept in the St. John's Church, as you like to call it. I went there to oversee the recovery operation."

"You mean someone got through the White House defenses of ferocious French Poodles and incredible high tech weapons?"

"I hate to admit it, but yes. And it wasn't just the poodles. We also have chihuahuas and shih tzus. I knew we shouldn't have relied on those foreign dogs. And the high tech weapons also failed - pea shooters, water pistols, and continuous playing of "It's a Small World After All."

"Whatever it was that was stolen from the Oval Office, was it in the church? Has it been recovered?"

"Unfortunately, it was not there."

"But what about the Bible, sir? You were holding up a Bible."

"Well, I couldn't very well stand there with nothing to say, nothing to do, and nothing to hold. I would have looked silly. So the Secret Service went into the church through the back entrance and retrieved my Bible."

"Excuse me, sir, you just said your Bible? I didn't know you kept a personal Bible in the church. Seems a bit out of character, if you will excuse my saying so."

"Yes, I do have a personal Bible and I keep it in that church. You think Melania would ever let me keep it in the East Wing? No way."

"Bible. Melania. East Wing. Church. Excuse me for being a bit slow on the uptake, sir, but what the fuck are you talking about?"

"I found that Bible in the bedside table of the hotel room when I was with Stormy Daniels. She even signed the inside cover: 'To my little, actually very little, Donald.' I have kept it as a souvenir."

"So you went to the church to retrieve an item stolen from the Oval Office by someone clever enough to evade French poodles, chihuahuas, shih tzus, pea shooters, water pistols and an infuriating Disney song. When the item wasn't there, you held aloft a Bible you found when you were with Stormy Daniels. But, sir, innocent, peaceful protesters lawfully exercising their First Amendment rights were dispersed with pepper spray, tear gas, and rubber bullets just so you could get to that church. Doesn't that bother you?"

"I've heard some dumb questions before, but never that dumb. Next question."

"We've heard that you were sequestered in the White House bunker for a while. Was that done for your safety?"

"Safety? Nah. I was never worried."

"Then what was the reason for your sequester?"

"Second time you used that word. Sequester. It means what?"

"It means that secret service agents carried a bawling, babbling, hysterical grown man into a room and locked the door."

"Well why didn't you just say so?"

"The reason, sir?"

"Actually, I'm not sure. I had lunch in the White House buffet room, with Gummy Bear. The chef focused on beans that day - baked beans, lima beans, pinto beans, kidney beans, black beans, mung beans, you get the point. And, boy, did I eat a lot. Then I was with Melania and Ivanka and they started screaming. Really hysterical. The secret service came in. The women huddled in the corner with the secret service guys and the next thing I know, the agents were saying "Yes, ma'am. We understand. Perfectly reasonable." And then I was rushed into the White House bunker."

"Changing the subject, sir. Have you invoked the Insurrection Act of 1807 and would you use it?"

"Yes, I invoked it and will use it if necessary. Furthermore, if that proves insufficient, I have already had discussions with NATO, President Putin, and President Xi to send their troops if needed."

"But do you really think all that force is necessary?'

"It will be if we don't find it."

"Huh? Find what?"

"The object that was taken from the Oval Office and turned out not to be in the church. Don't you remember I told you about that?"

"Yes, I remember. So it hasn't been found?"

"Not yet, but I will do everything within the power of the Presidency, even sending the US Military, plus NATO and the Russian and Chinese militaries, throughout the country, to recover it."

"What is it that could be so important, sir?"

"Someone took my ball swinging thingy from the Resolute Desk and I want it back!"

(With that, the President turns and starts to leave the Rose Garden. Sobs can be heard.)

Billy Bob and Bobbie Sue

(The new BOK Center in Tulsa, Oklahoma is packed with 6000 maniacal Trump fans. The decibel level exceeds that of a rock concert. Many of the attendees have already been there for hours. They are impatient for the big moment to arrive. The clock ticks as the President's campaign staff, supplemented by the Tulsa Police Dept., Oklahoma National Guard, Secret Service, and the elite K-9 corps of Des Moines, Iowa scramble to drag every last homeless and inebriated person to the BOK Center to fill the Upper Deck. The Trump fans already in the Upper Deck call it a night as the smell becomes overpowering.)

(The podium sits in the middle of the stage. The sides of the stage - the wings - are somewhat raised. Workmen are frantically trying to finish the handrails that lead down from both wings to the podium in the center. Carpentry complete, the painters put the finishing touches on "Make Handrails Great Again." It's Showtime!)

(And here comes the President, waving to his adoring fans. Steadfastly holding the handrails, he is assisted in his short, hesitant, mincing steps by two old ladies wearing "Grannies for Trump" tee shirts, each supporting one of his arms. The loudspeakers belt out "Twinkle Twinkle Little Star." Finally, the President arrives at the podium and the rally begins.)

"Welcome everybody and thank you for coming. I would have been here a few minutes earlier if those Do-Nothing Democrats hadn't iced down the stage and raised the wings when no one was looking. But I showed them when I sprinted the last ten paces. See? Even the grannies are huffing and puffing. One almost dropped her portable oxygen kit.

"First, I want to address the waiver of liability all of you were required to sign. This is not something I wanted to do, but there was simply no choice. The fault lies entirely with the Obama/Biden administration. You see, this arena is quite new. And like all arenas, it needed concession equipment. When they went to buy some, they learned, to their horror, that all new concession equipment manufacturing had moved offshore to Bolivia. Just another example of the sloppy Obama/Biden policies that cost American jobs. Maybe that's the real meaning of "Sloppy Joes."

(The crowd begins a chant of "Sloppy Joes, Sloppy Joes, Sloppy Joes," expelling viral particles with each refrain.)

"The developers of this arena, then, were forced to buy shoddy second-hand concession equipment. So who to blame for today's soggy hamburgers? Who to blame for those squishy french fries? Who to blame for those ketchup bottles that squirt only when pointed at your shirt? Who to blame?"

(Again, chants of "Sloppy Joes, Sloppy Joes.")

"That's right. Remember, when that concession guy hands you that disgustimundo burger or floppy hot dog, resist the temptation to shoot him. It's not his fault. And it's definitely not my fault. I take no responsibility for your gastrointestinal distress. Remember, you signed a waiver.

"Now I want to turn to something near and dear to my heart - voting. I expect all of you to vote in this next election."

(Excited whispers of "Hey ma, we're goin' to get to do that there votin' thing.")

"You've probably heard me say how bad it is to have mail-in voting. Well, guess what. I've changed my mind. Now, I'm all for it. Mike, you can wheel it out now."

(Vice President Pence wheels out from the wings a brand new, spiffy Xerox copier, accompanied by cries of "Spiffy, Spiffy" from the assembled masses.)

(Unfortunately, the Vice President loses his grip on the copier and it goes careening down the incline, smashing into the two grannies seated behind the President, waiting their turn to assist him away from the podium. The President takes no notice of the incident, although he does wonder what triggered the outbreak of "Sloppy Mike, Sloppy Mike".)

"This beautiful, brand new, spiffy Xerox copier can be yours. Everyone here who commits to vote by mail will have one of these beauties (the copiers, not the grannies) delivered to their home, complete with installation, instructions, and a ream of mail-in ballot quality copying paper. And it's yours to keep."

(Cheers erupt from the crowd as the paramedics attend to the grannies. One suffered a broken hip; the other only a few bruises, but her portable oxygen kit was crushed.)

"By the way, how did registration go for this rally? We used a new system."

(Mostly voices of satisfaction, but by no means unanimous.)

"If you had problems, and we know some of you did, blame Jared Kushner, not me. I take no responsibility."

(Whoops of "None, None, None" reverberate around the arena, carrying their viral particle payload.)

"Jared handles all of that technical, computer, internet stuff. He thought he was making things easier by requiring two names in the First Name field - like Billy Bob or Bubba John or Kathy Lee or Emma Sue. Reasonable decision, I think. After all, this is a Trump rally in Oklahoma. But he just didn't think about the few of you with only one measly, scrawny first name. In short, Jared was sloppy."

(Chants of "Sloppy Jared, Sloppy Jared," as viral particles wink at each other.)

"Now let me ask you a question. Think back to when you were in school. For those of you who never went to school, try to imagine being in school. Now think about Miss Biden - that ugly, mean, school-marmish spinster 6th grade teacher who everyone hated. Why did everyone hate her? Well, in addition to obvious character flaws like believing that people should be educated, she just loved to give tests. Tests. Tests. More tests. And you know what happened? The more tests she gave, the more of you she found to be dumber than a door knob.

"So what's the moral of this story? It's pretty obvious. If you stop testing, you stop the problem. Many of you here in this arena today wouldn't be the butt of jokes like "If he were any more stupid, he'd have to be watered twice a week," if old Miss Biden hadn't tested. So, as soon as I return to Washington, I will sign an Executive Order prohibiting any coronavirus test to be performed anywhere in the United States. No more tests, no more cases. No more cases, no more coronavirus. I personally will bring this shit to an end. And if some asshole, low-life Democrat governor wants to challenge this, he'll have the full power of the U.S. military yanking that swab out of the testee - and those soldiers will be yanking it from the ear side, not the nose."

(Crowd chants "Yank it out, Yank it out, Sloppy Joes, Sloppy Joes.")

"I want now to take you on a trip. We're going to Venice. You've all heard of Venice, right?"

(Many "Venice?" voices can be heard.)

"Come on, you know, where all the water slops over the sidewalks and the boatmen wear funny hats?"

(At first tentative, then more confident, shouts of "Sloppy water, Sloppy water" come in waves, with viral particles doing handstands on their wave riding surfboards, having a grand time.)

"Anyway, Venice is full of those wimpy Democrats and their piss ass accomplices the Fake News Media. For two weeks every year, they take over the city of Venice and force everyone to wear a mask. They even have the nerve to call it Carnevale. But on Shrove Tuesday, which we call Mardi Gras, our right-wing, gun-toting, anti-science, anti-mask, tattooed, double first-named Liberators storm in and put an end to these shenanigans and everyone flings off their mask. Let's hear it for the Giuseppe Tomasos of Venice coming to the rescue!"

(Shouts of "Giuseppe, Giuseppe" come from the left side of the arena while the President orchestrates "Tomato Sauce, Tomato Sauce" from the right.)

"So right now, when I count to three, we'll pretend we're in Venice at Mardi Gras and everyone - rip off your face mask. Ready? One...um...um...Two...um...um...umm...oh yeah...three!"

(Face masks fly. Well, at least from those homeless and inebriated "attendees" who seem to be the only ones wearing them. Several masks get jammed in the spiffy Xerox copier. People jump up and down. They hug each other. They kiss each other. They cough. They sneeze. They remember why they come to Trump rallies. And above all of this hullabaloo can be heard a faint whining noise - sort of a high-pitched "hehehe" sound emitted by whatever passes for the mouths of billions of tiny coronavirus particles. Tiny coronavirus particles that didn't even have to register, nor be dragged in.)

(All of a sudden, the President abruptly ends his participation in the rally. He waves to the crowd. He hesitates, then hesitates some more. Finally, two seeing eye dogs - replacements for the two Xerox copier grannie victims - race to the podium and hold out their paws. They escort the President off the stage. He trips only once on a stray MAGA mask.)

(Why the sudden exit? The President had just realized that his advance team forgot to bring all ten prophylactic doses of hydroxychloroquine to Tulsa. Faced with the choice of cheating 6,000 rabid followers out of their money's worth or missing a dose or two of hydroxychloroquine, the President simply left (to the rousing strains of "If You're Happy and You Know It Clap Your Hands.").

(Ed. postscript - The Tulsa rally went down in history as the world's largest coronavirus super spreader event. Eventually, the entire state of Oklahoma went into lockdown. When asked about his role in it later, the President was heard to remark: "Me? I don't have the virus".)

Yes We're Going to a Party, Party

(The occupant of the bedroom, awake since 4:00 am, finally sheds his pajamas - the ones with toy trains - and dons his best party outfit.)

"Damn, damn, damn. Where is my cone birthday party hat?"

(He rummages through drawers, tossing clothes behind him, until he finally finds it hidden behind six bottles of Lysol, all in different colors.)

(After 20 minutes of hopping around the bedroom in uncontrolled excitement, he makes his way to the Oval Office, where the party is due to begin at 10:00 am.)

"I wonder what I'm going to get this year. I hope I get another voodoo doll of Nancy Pelosi. I stuck so many pins in that one it fell apart. Hopefully no more ties, though."

(The President busies himself with his ball swinging thingy until 9:45 am, when the guests for the President's birthday party begin to arrive.)

"Happy birthday, Mr. President. Under your strong leadership, another year has passed." (Vice President Pence)

"Happy birthday, Mr. President. We've managed to limit the stimulus payments to $1200, a great achievement." (Treasury Secretary Mnuchin).

"Happy birthday, Mr. President. I'm pleased to report Federal law enforcement made 186,734 arrests yesterday." (Attorney General

William Barr, wearing a Hawaiian aloha shirt and dancing the boogaloo.)

"Happy b..."

"OK, stop, stop. Enough already. I get the point. I want my presents!"

(Everyone heads over to the corner of the room where a very large pile of wrapped presents lies.)

"Kellyanne, I'm putting you in charge of the presents. Pick one, announce who it's from, tear off the wrapping paper, hold the present up for all to see and proclaim what it is. Got it?"

"Got it, sir. But why not put Vice President Pence in charge"?

"Are you kidding? He's so OCD he'll take forever to unwrap the presents and then he'll want to fold the wrapping paper into origami cranes."

"Why not Attorney General Barr?"

"OK, let's take a vote. Raise your hand if you ever want to see Bill Barr dance the boogaloo again........I thought so."

"Alright, I'll do it.

1st present. "I'll start with this one from..."

"Me! It's from me. Me." (says the Vice President)

"Yes, indeed it is." (says Kellyanne). "And look how meticulously it's wrapped. Let's see what it is... Oh goodness, you're going to love this, sir. It's a Bible with the word "Front" on the front, "Back" on the back, and "This Edge Up" pointing to the top."

"How thoughtful, Mike. How thoughtful."

2nd present. "From Melania, sir. Mrs. Trump, would you like to open it?"

"No, I already know it vat is. You open."

"Let's see here... It's extra heavy duty deodorant called "For Pits Sake!" Says that it's especially effective for Slovenian pig farmers and people who smell like them."

<u>3rd present</u>. "I'll continue. Well, this one is a surprise. The card says it's from General Mattis, sir."

"Actually, I'm not surprised. Those military types understand discipline and understand who's in charge and understand obedience, tough obedience. What did he get me?"

"It's an annotated copy of the U.S. Constitution, sir."

"Better move on, Kellyanne."

<u>4th present</u>. "Oh look at this nice one with the fancy red wrapping paper... Yes, just as I thought. It's postmarked Beijing and it's from President Xi himself."

"How thoughtful. Open it Kellyanne. The suspense is killing me."

"Why, it's a framed first edition of the new one page US-China trade deal you just negotiated. It's signed by President Xi himself in both hanyu (characters) and hanyu pinyin (romanization of Chinese characters)."

"Wow! What a great present! Read the treaty for us, Kellyanne."

"It says: "We sell, you buy.""

"I told everyone I was tough on China. See?"

<u>5th present</u>. "I'm not sure I want to open this next one."

"Oh, go ahead. And don't tell us who it's from. I want to guess."

"Alright, sir... Well, it looks like a paper jigsaw puzzle, but there's no picture to guide us. Only lots and lots of small jagged-edged pieces of paper."

"Hmmm. That surely is odd. I wonder who it could be from. Is there a card?"

"No, sir. No, wait. Yes, I found the card."

"Then read it."

"My dear Donald. I know you were upset when I ripped up your State of the Union speech. I'm returning it now. You are always in my prayers. Nancy."

"What a horrible present. That woman knows I'm no good at jigsaw puzzles."

6th present. "This next one looks like a gift box of Turkish delights. No, wait a minute. It's a box of Syrian delights - basbousa (semolina cakes), baklava, and ma'amoul (date filled cookies). Scrumptious."

"But who's it from? Me and Assad aren't exactly buddies, you know."

"There's a card. It's from Turkish President Erdoğan. He says "The food is great here. Thanks for the invite. Got rid of all the Kurds, by the whey."

7th present. "This next one we know will be good. It's from the Attorney General. Let's see... A Hawaiian aloha shirt, hip hop dance sneakers, and a boombox."

(Bill Barr goes over to the boombox, turns it on, and starts his boogaloo, inviting the President to join him.)

"Security! Security! Secret Service! Where are you? You're supposed to protect us!"

(The Attorney General is escorted out the door, boogying all the way.)

8th present. "And here is one addressed to "Donald John MacLeod Trump." Weird. Why two last names?"

"I can answer that, Kellyanne." (Secretary of State Pompeo interjects, drawing upon his international expertise.) "In the Spanish tradition, a person customarily takes on the surname of his or her mother as well as the father. The mother's surname precedes the father's surname. Because the President's mama was Mary Anne MacLeod, his name becomes Donald John MacLeod Trump in the Spanish tradition."

"That's fascinating, Mike. I knew there was a reason I picked you for Secretary of State. On which of your official international trips did you pick up this information?"

"None of them, sir. I've just gotten to be good buddies with Rodrigo, the owner of Rodrigo's Uruguayan Taco Shack in Embassy Row. I go there a few times a week. You should try it."

"I will. But how about we open my presents first?"

"I'm on it, sir." (Kellyanne). "Hmmm. This one's a multicolored Lego kit for building a wall. And there's a card from Mexican President Andres Manuel Lopez Obrador. The card says: "Go ahead and build your steenking wall with this. And here's the receipt for $22.61. I expect to be reimbursed."

9th present. "Oh look at this lovely couple on the wrapping paper. I wonder who they are?"

(Director of National Intelligence John Ratcliffe chimes in.)

"That's Twitter CEO Jack Dorsey and his faithful sidekick Jennifer, the Twitter switchboard operator. We've had them under surveillance ever since they launched a subsidiary called Black Birds matter. It seems that the supporters of Magic Johnson in the long-standing debate concerning who was better - Larry Bird (inspiration for the Twitter mascot Larry the Bird) or Magic Johnson - were making rumbling noises about racial discrimination, especially since the Twitter mascot is blue."

"I'll open the present anyway... It looks like a disk with some software. The note from Jack and Jennifer explains that it's the latest and most comprehensive spell checker software designed specifically for Twitter users."

"Well that's wunderful. But why send it to me?"

10th present. "Oh daddy, the next present is from me. Can I open it?"

"Of course, Snuzzlepuff."

"Here. See? It's a brand new, shiny ball swinging thingy. And it's monogrammed. Each ball has one letter from your last name: T-R-U-M-P."

"Fantastic, dear. Come here so I can give you a big ~~feel~~ hug. What's next?"

11th present. "Oops. This next one comes from Ambassador John Bolton and it feels like a book. No, wait a minute, it feels like two books. Do you want me to open it?"

"Of course, a present is a present. And furthermore, I can't remember the last time I actually felt a book, let alone try to read one. Let's see what it is."

"Just like I thought – two books. The first one is the Ambassador's new book, "The Room Where It Happened," autographed by John Bolton himself. And there's an inscription – "No disinfecting the stuff in here. Time to shine that all powerful sunlight into the darkest corners." The second book seems to be some sort of dictionary – "A Beginner's Guide to English Words."

"Well, you can say one thing for John. At least he didn't forget my birthday."

12th present. "Ah, sir. From our very own Dr. Ben Carson. Let's see. It's a brightly colored shawl, or scarf, or mantle, or shoulder wrap, or... Just what is it, Ben?"

"It's a kente cloth scarf. From the Asanti tradition in what is now modern day Ghana. A symbol of Africanness. But look further, Kellyanne."

"Oh, there's another one. And another. And... How many are there, Ben?"

"There are 17 in total. One for the President and one for each Cabinet secretary and the Vice President."

(The President chimes in.)

"They're beautiful. But why? And please tell me you're not changing your name to Kunta Kinte."

"I figured if kente was good enough for the Democrats, it's got to be even better for the Republicans. And I'll be damned if it won't look better even on our very own sourpuss Wilbur Ross than it looked on Pelosi."

(The President again.)

"Right at ya on that, bro. Ol' Wilbur gonna think he be Diana Ross, not no honky Wilbur Ross. Shake me a little buzzsaw. Down in the hood with my nieces and nephews. Gettin' down with the crawdads. Right on."

(Quizzical glances are exchanged.)

13th present. "Sir, this next one is from Joe Biden. Do you want me to open it?"

"Of course. He might be sleepy, but he actually is a really nice guy. That's probably why he loses all the time. Let's see what it is, Kellyanne."

"Oh, how lovely. It's a snow globe with the Oval Office and Resolute Desk inside. Let me shake it."

"I hope you're referring to the snow globe, Kellyanne. Remember, we already threw out Attorney General Barr for shaking his booty. Give it here."

(The President looks, shakes, and approves.)

"I told you he was a nice guy. Is that a card, Kellyanne? Read it, please."

"My dear Mr. President. Jill and I would like to offer you our heartiest best wishes for a most happy birthday. Although I have seen a few more of them than you have, at this point, who's really counting. We wanted to get you something that will help you remember the room you're in now, as we can imagine how quickly memories will fade come January 20."

14th present. "You can bring it in now." (Kellyanne calls to the White House butler. He, assisted by some others, brings into the room and places on the Resolute Desk several boxes full of Georgetown Cupcakes.)

"Oh goodie, goodie, goodie" (exclaims the President with drool dripping down his face, leaving ugly streaks of orange). "I want the Cookies & Cream Birthday Fudge and Vegan Apple Cinnamon. And then maybe Gluten-Free Strawberry Lava Fudge."

"Vegan? Gluten-Free?" (everyone chimes in at once)

15th present. "Wait, before we eat, there's one more present. This one looks like it's the last one. Let me see. Just a card."

"Read it, Kellyanne."

"My dearest Mr. President. I cannot overstate my appreciation for what you have done for me over the past five months. To show my gratitude, I am sending, under separate cover, 5 million mail-in ballots, pre-cast for Donald Trump, for your use in Michigan, Wisconsin, and Pennsylvania on November 3. After all, if you win, I win."

"Huh? Who's it from?"

"Don't know, sir. All it says is: "With kindest birthday wishes, C.V."

"Well, even though we don't know who sent it, it's clearly the best present yet."

"It looks like that's all the presents, Mr. President. You did very well this year."

(Everyone applauds and heads for the cupcakes.)

(But at that very moment, the doorbell rings at the front entrance to the White House. Upon opening the door, the White House valet sees a man dressed in one of those black and purple Federal Express uniforms.)

"Howdy, sir. I've got a Fed Ex delivery for someone named "Trumplethinskin. Address is 1600 Pennsylvania Avenue. Am I in the right place?"

"You are, indeed, Mr.... I'm sorry, I didn't catch your name."

"You all can just call me "Squishie."

"Squishie, sir, your name is "Squishie?"

"Old nickname from when the local police squished me into a trash can. Name kinda stuck."

"Very good, sir. I'll deliver the package for you. Is it that large sack over there behind you?"

"It is, but my instructions are to hand deliver the package myself and ol' Squishie always follows instructions."

"Very well, Mr. Squishie. Follow this corridor. Take a left just past the men's room. When you see the portrait of Jared Kushner, remember there is a puke receptacle just to its right. Go about 20 paces further and the Oval Office is straight ahead."

(In front of the portrait of Jared Kushner, with a completely full puke receptacle just to its right, Squishie comes across a disconsolate Attorney General Barr.)

"Hey, bro, why the long face? This is some pretty bad ass place."

"I know, but I was thrown out of the party."

"Why?"

"I guess they didn't like my boogaloo dance."

"Show me your moves, bro. I've got my boombox right here."

(Squishie plays some music; Attorney General Barr dances.)

"Man, you're lucky they didn't ship you off to Finland and take away your passport. That is horrendous. That is some nasty bad shit. And I don't mean nasty bad shit like good nasty bad shit. I mean nasty bad shit like baaad nasty bad shit. You look like that scarecrow guy in Wizard of Oz with half his stuffing missing who got caught right in front of some big ass fancy Dyson fan or some similar contraption. How 'bout I show you some moves?"

"That would be great."

(The two of them - Squishie and the Attorney General - start boogying right in front of the Jared Kushner portrait, blocking access to the puke receptacle. The Attorney General proves to be a fast learner.)

"I gotta deliver this package now. Why don't you come with me?"

(The door to the Oval Office opens and the party-goers are treated to the sight of Squishie and the Attorney General break dancing to the sounds of Boogey Fever.)

"My bud here has some more presents for you, Mr. President."

"In that case, you're forgiven, Bill...barely."

"I have to deliver this personally to a Trumplethinskin."

"That would be me." (says the President eagerly)

"Are you sure? It says "Trumplethinskin, not Trumpleorangepeel."

"Just give it here and you can leave."

"Just need a signature, Mr. Orange Julius."

(President signs. On his way out, Squishie calls out to the Attorney General: "See ya Tuesday for your next lesson.")

(Some weird, convoluted hand gesture from the Attorney General in reply.)

(The President takes the final present, the one personally delivered by Squishie.)

"I'll open this last one myself. Let's see here... Huh? A sack full of very nasty presents, topped off with a Biden 2020 cap. And a nasty card. Plus a rather thick envelope with a manuscript inside called the "Oh Daddy Chronicles." WTF? It's all postmarked from a place called The Villages in Florida."

"Don't you remember, sir? That's the place with all the old people who can't afford to live on the coast. They drive around in golf carts and play something called pickleball. You were there last year."

"Oh, yes. Now I remember. Owned by the Morse family. Filthy rich. Big Republican donors. Hot looking daughter. My kind of people. But this can't be tolerated. Kellyanne, get me Mark Morse on the phone. Now."

"Good morning. This is Mark Morse, the richest man in Florida's Friendliest Hometown. How can I help you to make me even richer? Interested in a new alligator villa? Or what about a bonsai bungalow? We even have a few brand new designer homes just south of Orlando. And the golf cart superhighway we're building to connect that section to Brownwood will have eight rest stops, one of them complete with hotel, spa and bingo room."

"Mark, stop. This is Donald Trump. We have serious business to discuss."

"Sorry, Mr. President. I get carried away when I smell other people's money. I think you understand."

"I do, I do. But I just received a nasty birthday card and nasty presents from a subversive group calling themselves the ODCC - the Oh Daddy Chronicles Community. And they seem to be largely located in The Villages. I'll have Kellyanne contact you shortly with names (or at least initials) and details. But right now I want to know what actions you plan to take against these degenerates."

"Well, for starters, I'll code their Villages IDs so that it's impossible for them to get reliable, super-fast Wi-Fi in the rec centers. Second, I'll take away their ability to get that 5% discount we offer to early birds who are dumb enough to pay $50 for reserved seats and a watered down drink with no pink parasol at one of our stupid holiday celebrations, like the one we have for National Dust Mop Day. Finally, there is our new money- sucking idea inspired by the coronavirus."

"That sounds interesting. Tell me about it."

"Well, we no longer have free live music in the evenings because of social distancing problems. So what we're going to do is allow people to drive their golf cart onto the grounds of the polo fields, sit there for 90 minutes sweating their butts off and getting eaten alive by mosquitoes, no place to pee unless you dodge your way through all the golf carts to get to the one in-service port-a-potty, and listen to the same music you used to be able to listen to for free. All this for only $40 per person."

"So you'll punish these despicable ODCC people by refusing to sell them tickets?"

"Hell no. We'll force them to *buy* tickets."

"Well, Mark. It sounds like you're on top of things, so I'll leave it you and Kellyanne to work out the details. Bye."

(The party continued until Bill Barr decided to practice some of the moves he learned from Squishie. Then everyone left.)

Moniker Mayhem

(Senator Bernie Sanders, Senator Elizabeth Warren, Senator Mitch McConnell, Treasury Secretary Steve Mnuchin, Housing and Urban Development Secretary Dr. Ben Carson, New York Governor Andrew Cuomo, and First Daughter Ivanka Trump file into the White House Cabinet Room. White House Chief of Staff Mark Meadows is there to greet them.)

"Thank you all for coming. As you know, all of you have agreed to be a member of the We Need a New Fucking Name for This Here Army Base Task Force. I am the chair of that Task Force. The person who came up with the name for the Task Force was not invited to be on it, for obvious reasons. Each of you has been asked to propose three names for the Army bases, as the initial assignment for this Task Force is a pilot project for Forts Benning, Hood, and Bragg. I have been informed that all of you have come prepared with your proposed names. Correct?"

(Seven heads nod in agreement.)

"We will proceed as follows. When I call on you, you will read the names you propose. When everyone has spoken, we will have discussion. The proposed names and the minutes of the discussion will be provided to the President, who will make the final decision. Steve, you first."

"Thank you, Mr. Chairman. My proposed names are:

"Fort Pierpont Morgan"

"Fort Rothschild"

"Fort Soros"

I'm sure the President will be pleased with all of these, as they reek of money."

"Thank you, Treasury Secretary Mnuchin. Next, I'd like to turn to Ivanka Trump. Please go ahead."

"Thank you wank you Markie. Can I call you Markie? Here is what I came up with while having my nails done:

"Fort Poppy"

"Fort Zosia"

"Fort Cassia"

"I know these are girls' names, and I'm not so sure that Daddykins will like them, but they're just so cutesy wutesy. That's all."

"We appreciate the effort, Ivanka. Now we turn to the other side of the aisle. Governor Cuomo, what say you, paisan?"

"Thank you, Chairman. My choices are rather straightforward and shouldn't generate any controversy:

"Fort Giuseppe"

"Fort Alonzo"

"Fort Luciano"

Capiche?"

"Si, capiche. Next up is Senator Sanders. Please, sir, the floor is yours."

"Before I give my suggestions, let me first say that this whole naming system is rigged. It benefits only the top 1% of names and ignores the hard work and toil of all the names under it. And furthermore, I demand that the minimum word length in a name be increased from the present three letters to at least six letters so that the name doesn't just disappear from the tongue before having a chance to be alive. These are names we're talking about, not inanimate objects."

"Are you finished, Senator?"

"Yes. Here are my name suggestions:

"Fort Health Care for All"

"Fort Minimum Wage"

"Fort Let Me Just Say This"

"Thank you so much, Senator. Could you remind us how the hell you got on this Task Force? But let's move on. I recognize our distinguished Secretary of Housing and Urban Development, and the only black American on this Task Force, Dr. Ben Carson. Ben, the floor is yours."

"Thank you, Mr. Chairman. First, let me say how honored I am to serve on this Task Force with all you honky over privileged white folk. But let me get to the point. Here are my choices:

"Fort BLM1"

"Fort BLM2"

"Fort BLM3"

"Thank you so much, Ben, for your refreshing contribution. But I am forced to wonder whether the President will look favorably on naming forts after Black Lives Matter."

"I've considered that. I think all we have to do is tell him that "BLM" stands for "Boise League of Masturbators." That's probably something he can relate well to."

"Boise?" (Senator Sanders reaches for his wallet and pulls out what appears to be a membership card.) "Mine says "Burlington."

"I think we'd better move on now. Next, I give the floor to the honkiest of honkies, Senate Majority Leader Mitch McConnell. Mitch?"

"John, Harry, Pete"

"Thank you, Senator. Very thought provoking, very insightful. Lastly, we will hear from Senator Elizabeth Warren. Please proceed."

"Thank you, Chairman Meadows. When I was informed that I would be serving on this Task Force, I immediately developed a plan for how I would go about the naming decision and for how I would react to other name suggestions that I might not fully agree with. I planned to steadfastly follow the plan. However, I forgot to write it down and I forgot it. So I am winging it here today. My suggestions are:

"Fort Ahyoka"

"Fort Guatemoc"

"Fort Matoskah"

I hope you will forgive me for using the names of certain of my Indian moccasins." (more than a few strange looks in her direction) "What? Doesn't everyone name their moccasins?"

(Task Force Chairman Meadows conducts the discussion phase of the meeting. About four hours later, the meeting adjourns.)

(One week later. Everyone gathers again for a lunch meeting in the Cabinet Room. President Donald Trump is also in attendance. He speaks.)

"I want to thank everyone for all the hard work they put into this assignment, and especially to Chief of Staff Meadows for getting everything to run smoothly in this contentious topic. Please, everyone, continue to enjoy your Waldorf salad. It looks delicious. I'll get to mine in a second.

"I have made my decision for the new names to be given to Forts Benning, Hood, and Bragg. Here they are:

"Fort Donald"

"Fort Eric"

"Fort Barron"

(All at once, eight plates of half-eaten Waldorf salads go hurtling across the room in the direction of the Orange One.)

Riddle Me This, Batman

(The President enters an examination room at Walter Reed National Military Medical Center.)

"Welcome to the cognitive abilities section of Walter Reed, Mr. President. My name is Dr. Somchai Sonjohnkoksoong. I'll be asking you just a few rather simple questions to gauge whether there is any impairment in your cognitive abilities. It's a standard test and nothing to be concerned about. Of course, if you can repeat my name right now, we can safely conclude the examination without going any further. Care to try?"

"I could repeat it easily, but this exam should be fun. Let's go ahead and, Dr. Something Somethingscooking, get ready to be impressed."

"I'm sure I will be, sir. First, can you state your full name?"

"Donald John Trump."

"And your date of birth."

"June 14, 1946."

"Excellent. And what day of the week is it today?"

"Hmm. Tuesday? Friday? You know, I just can't remember. That's how it goes with this pandemic thing - every day feels like every other day. Isn't that so?"

"Yes, that is a common cognitive phenomenon, but only for those people whose routines have been either disrupted or eliminated by the current situation. People continuing in their regular job do not experience that issue. And you, certainly, have a regular job that should keep you quite busy."

"So you're saying that my going into work might help with this day of the week thing? I'll have to look into that."

"Let's move on to math. It's Election Day. The results are in. Joe Biden receives 304 electoral college votes and you receive 234 electoral college votes. Who is the winner?"

"First of all, I don't answer silly hypothalamus questions. But if I did, I'd point out that Biden's total is the result of fraudulent voting on a massive scale. I know this because my campaign delivered over a million mail-in ballot copying machines to my base." (Ed. note - see episode entitled "Billy Bob and Bobbie Sue.") "So the answer to your question is that I won the election."

"Hmm. Interesting. Well, the next area is science. Are you ready?"

"Sure am. I had an uncle who went to MIT. Made it through his sophomore year."

"Er, yes, thank you for sharing. Imagine that medical researchers conduct a double-blind placebo controlled clinical trial to determine the effectiveness of hydroxychloroquine in treating COVID-19."

"Why would they do that? Everyone knows it works."

"This is just a hypothetical, OK? You do know what a placebo is, correct?"

"Of course, do you think I'm an idiot? "Placebo" is the name of that Italian opera singer who some people think was better than Pavaroni."

"Umm, I'm not sure where to begin here. First of all, it's Pavarotti - Luciano Pavarotti - not Pavaroni. Secondly, the other opera singer you are referring to is Placido - Placido Domingo - not

Placebo. And he's Spanish, not Italian. Are you sure you want to continue? I think I already have enough material for my report."

"Stop now? No way. This is fun. And now I do remember about "placebo." It's how you say "thank you" in Russian. Vladimir taught it to me."

"Well, the Russian word is "spasiba," but let's continue with the clinical trial. Let's assume that 100 COVID-19 patients are given hydroxychloroquine and 100 patients are given a placebo. In the hydroxychloroquine group, 17 people show clear clinical improvement. In the control group (receiving only a recording of Nessun Dorma sung by Pavarotti), 26 people show clear clinical improvement. Based on these results, what conclusion can you reach regarding the efficacy of hydroxychloroquine as a treatment modality for COVID-19?"

"Conclusion? That's easy. It clearly works - and powerfully."

"Well, sir, could you explain how you reached that conclusion? After all, more people improved without hydroxychloroquine than with it."

"Simple. Peter Navarro wrote a 96 page memo on the subject."

"And you've read the entire memo?"

"Me? Are you kidding? Hell no. He just summarized it for me."

"And his summary?"

"It works."

"OK. I think we might need one more science question. Assume you have a Newton's Cradle. I believe you refer to this device as a "ball swinging thingy.""

"I know it well. Use it all the time. This one is going to be a piece of cake. Shoot."

"Assume you take the two left balls of the Newton's Cradle, hold them at a distance to the other three balls, then release the two balls. What happens to the balls of the Newton's Cradle upon impact?"

"Huh? You can do the ball swinging thingy with more than one ball? Wow. Who would have thought?"

"Let's move on to the use of the English language."

"Great. One of my many strongly points. You know, I had an uncle who went to MIT."

"I'm sure he did. Probably even made it through his sophomore year."

"He did. How did you know that?"

"Let's keep going - use of the English language. I'd like to read to you one of your recent tweets. You then tell me what is wrong with it. OK?"

"Go rightly ahead."

"Saddened to hear the news of civil rights hero John Lewis passing. Melania and I send our prayers to he and his family."

"I remember that one. The entire White House staff was pushing me to say something, so I did. Otherwise, meh."

"Perhaps, but there is one obvious mistake in that short tweet. Can you identify it?"

"Uhhh... John Lewis wasn't a hero?"

(The doctor shakes his head no.)

"Melania didn't really give a shit?"

(Same shake of the head.)

"I didn't give a shit?"

"Probably not, but that's not what I had in mind. Give it one more try."

"Hmmm. I've got it. I don't know any prayers - other than the one asking that all inner city voting machines break down on election day - so how could I be sending prayers to he and his family?"

"I'm afraid that's not it, either. Here it is. The word "he" should be used in the subjective case. You used it in the objective case. I think grammarians would refer to that as a "no-no.""

"Well, I disagree. And if you want to check with someone with a lot of erduition with words, give a call to Professor Matthew Bevis at Keble College, University of Oxford. He, Kellyanne, and I had a great phone conversation a while back. And he knows a lot about words. Even wrote a book about them - something called "Wordsworth's Fun." All about words. Lots of them. Powerful words, strong words, beautiful words, fun words. He'll tell you I'm right. Just don't ask him about quark unless you want to hear about Shakespeare and shit and a book no one can read." (Ed. note - see episode entitled "Amazing Quark.")

"I'll do that. Now we move on to the penultimate part of the exam. I'm going to show you several drawings and I want you to reproduce what you see, using the papers in front of you. Alright?"

"Actually, not alright. All you've given me are #2 pencils. I only use crayons or, sometimes, a black sharpie. How about giving me a sharpie in case your drawings include the state of Alabama?"

(A black sharpie is provided to the President.)

"Ready for the first drawing?"

"Actually, no. This paper won't work. It's too thick."

"Too thick? I can assure you that it's standard writing paper. No one has ever complained about it. Why don't you just give it a try?"

"No, no, I won't give it a try! It's too thick! It's too thick!"

"Please calm down, sir, and tell me what kind of paper you would like."

"I need normal tracing paper, of course, if you want me to reproduce your drawings. I have a huge supply in the Resolute Desk in the Oval Office. Maybe my staff could helicopter over there and get some."

"I think we can safely skip this portion of the exam."

"Are we finished then?"

"Almost. Just one more cognitive challenge, sir. And I must warn you that some people find this one rather difficult. Are you ready?"

"You bet I am."

"OK. I'm going to ask you six questions. Once you have answered all of them correctly, then you must repeat those six answers/words in the correct order without hesitation. Understand?"

"Can't wait."

"1st question. What is the 15th letter of the English alphabet?"

(The President begins to count on his fingers, while mouthing the letters.)

"Got it. It's "o"."

"Correct."

"2nd question. Tell me the last name of the Secretary of the Interior during the Reagan Administration."

"Watt. James Watt. A true hero to all of us anti-environmentalists."

"Correct and very impressive. 3rd question. What is the indefinite article in the English language that is used before a consonant?"

(The President is thinking.)

"A...... Just a second... A...."

"Correct again. It's the letter "a." Now for the 4th question. I will show you a picture of a barnyard animal and you tell me what it is. And here's a hint - it's not an elephant."

(The President scrutinizes the picture with some consternation. Then he remembers one of his tracings from the previous week. His face lights up, looking like one of those jack-o-lanterns lit with a candle on the inside at Halloween.)

"I know that animal. It's a goose."

"Right you are, sir. The 5th question is pretty easy. With what organ of the body do we see?"

""Eye."

"Yes, much too easy for you, sir. Now for the 6th and last question. What is another name for a sweet potato?"

(Blank look on the President's face.)

"Let me give you a hint. You can find the word from one of Popeye's famous sayings - "I am what I am and that's all that I am." Say it fast."

"I can't do that. Where's my corn cob pipe?"

"Try it without the pipe. Just this once."

"OK. Here goes. And I'll say it fast. "I yam what I yam and that's all that I yam."

"Great, sir. The word we were looking for is, indeed, "yam." Now the real cognitive challenge is for you to repeat all six answers, in the proper order. I'll give you a few seconds to organize your thoughts. Tell me when you're ready."

(The President spends a short time thinking and then indicates he's ready.)

"I'm going to time this so begin when I say go... Ready? Go."

"O........Watt........A.........Goose........Eye........Yam."

"You're going to need to do it more quickly, sir. Without hesitation. Ready? Go."

"O Watt A Goose Eye Yam"

"Perfect, Mr. President. I couldn't have said it better myself. And I think we can end the examination on that note."

So we're done?"

"We are, sir.

"What's the highest score you can get?"

"35 points, sir."

"I bet I got around 40, right?"

"Not quite, sir."

"Well, then, what's my score?"

"-7, sir. And that's only because I graded charitably."

"What are you writing now? Is that my certificate of incredible achievement?"

"It's a school voucher good for three days a week at the Marymount School for the Hopelessly Challenged Mental Midgets. You're actually in luck because they're open despite the pandemic. Just be sure to bring your own lunch."

(The President gets up to leave...and walks into a wall.).

EPISODE XXVII

Sikh and Ye Shall Find

(The door to the Oval Office opens and in walks former South Carolina governor and U.S. Ambassador to the United Nations, Nikki Haley.)

"Wow, Nikki Haley, now there's a sight for sore eyes."

"Good morning, Mr. President. I hope you don't mind my intrusion."

"Not at all. And I'm pleased to see you're not wearing a mask. By the way, that's a lovely sari you have on today. When did you start going ethnic?"

"About six months ago when I became pen pals with Joshadaben Modi - you know, Prime Minister Modi's wife. And since then, we've been exchanging TikTok dance videos."

"Uh huh... And, yes, I remember Jishepoienieoubn quite well. It was her that I puked on when I first learned of Dr. Vaccine's statement to the press. And your sari does now look rather familiar."

"Dr. Vaccine, sir?"

"You know, the one whose name sounds almost exactly like that messenger RNA vaccine Moderna is working on. I think her name is Nancy Messonnier."

"Right sir."

"Now don't tell me you're going to put one of those dots on your forehead as part of this ethnic thing, are you?"

"Not a chance, sir. Those dots, technically called a "bindi" are part of the Hindu and Jain traditions. I am a Sikh."

"And since your name is Nikki, not Jane, I guess we're OK." (President chortles at his cleverness.)

"So, Nikki, tell me why you're here."

"Well, it sort of has to do with Stacey Abrams."

"You mean that fat black bitch from Georgia who wants to be Sleepy Joe's vice presidential running mate and is aggressively telling everyone about it?"

"That's the one, although, as a woman, I quarrel with your characterization of her. Anyway, I see her as sort of an inspirational figure - a woman who knows what she wants and is not shy about asking for it. I am here now, sir, to tell you that I want the same thing."

"You want to be Sleepy Joe's running mate? You've got to be kidding. Besides, he already has one Indian wannabe trying out for the job. And why are you telling me? Shouldn't you be telling Sleepy Joe (between naps, of course)?"

"I think you misunderstood, sir. My fault, I've been out of your Administration for a while now and I forgot what level of discourse is required for clear communication with you. No, I have no interest in being former Vice President and all-around nice guy Joe Biden's vice presidential running mate. I want to be your vice presidential running mate in the 2020 election."

"But what about Vice President Pence?"

"He's boring."

"Right on that."

"He's afraid of women."

"Double right on that."

"He sounds like a recording."

"Can't argue there."

"He looks like a cigar store Indian when standing in the background."

"Agreed, but with impeccably coiffed white hair."

"He has been seen wearing a mask."

"Unforgivable."

"And he's a card carrying member of the International Ass Lickers Society."

"Subversive international group probably dominated by China."

"So, are you planning to take action?"

"I'm going to act strongly, and powerfully, and hugely, and massively, and beautifully, did I say forcefully? He's gone - history, on the ash heaps, gonzo, hasta la vista baby. After all, I am the all-powerful, super macho President... By the way, Nikki, would you mind telling him?"

"Not at all, Mr. President."

"But now let's not get ahead of ourselves, though. Just because I have decided in a matter of less than one minute to boot Mike Pence from the ticket, that doesn't mean I'm giving the job to you. I first have to conduct extensive due diligence. After all, with a 74 year-old morbidly obese man who takes hydroxychloroquine against all competent medical advice as President, the vice president has to be ready and able to step in at a moment's notice."

"Of course, sir. I would expect no less. But with my educational background, business experience, executive experience as a governor, and diplomatic accomplishments at the United Nations, I feel confident I can handle whatever challenging questions you might pose to me."

"Excellent. I take up the challenge. First category - intelligence.

"What is your favorite color?"

"Blue, sir."

"Excellent. What is your favorite animal?"

"Bengal tiger, sir, they're very powerful."

"Excellent again. What is your favorite food?"

"Aloo shimla mirch."

"Uh. Maybe you could try again."

"Sorry, how about hari matar ka nimona?"

"I don't think you're getting this, Nikki. Try something truly American, like Chinese take-out."

"OK. My favorite food is Chinese take-out."

"Excellent. What is your favorite movie?"

"Sholay. It was voted best Bollywood movie of all time. GOAT. Number one. All-time best. Nothing better. Just like you, sir. I'm sure you would love it."

"You've passed the intelligence portion of the vetting process. So far so good. Now we go to coronavirus. Ready?"

"All set, Mr. President."

"Can the coronavirus be seen from Outer Space?"

"Not a chance, sir. It's invisible."

"Is the coronavirus friendly?"

"It's an enemy, sir, most definitely."

"Excellent. Did the coronavirus result from an experiment in the Wuhan Virology Lab in China?"

"Most assuredly, sir. If it had come from a bat, it wouldn't be able to find people to infect. Bats are blind, sir." (Ed. note - not true.)

"Huh. I hadn't considered that evidence. Excellent observation, Nikki. And now, one last question having to do with coronavirus. If you test negative, how do you relay that to the Fake News press?"

"Why, I would say: "I tested very positively in another sense. So this morning, I tested positively toward negative, right? So, no, I tested perfectly this morning, meaning I tested negative. But that's a way of saying it, positively toward the negative."

"Wow. Could you repeat that slowly? I want to write it down."

"Certainly, sir. Could I ask one question?"

"Of course, fire away."

"Well, if you re-open the country very quickly as you are trying to do, aren't more people likely to die, thus raising the death statistic?"

"You are absolutely right. I thought about that question for several weeks and came to the same conclusion. I even ran my insight by Fauci and he agreed I was on to something. But after another five minutes thought, I realized that dead people don't show up in the unemployment statistics, so I think we're actually ahead of the game here."

"Interesting way of looking at it. Do you have any more questions for me, Mr. President?"

"I think we have covered more than enough ground for the vetting process. I am totally satisfied that I should dump puritan Mike and enter the election with you as my vice presidential candidate. The job is yours. I'll call Brad Parscale, my campaign manager, right away to get him started on churning out all of the new "Trump/Haley" campaign paraphernalia. And I might even invoke the Defense Production Act if we need more production capacity. Damn, this is exciting!"

"Oh, Mr. President, I forgot to mention one thing, now that this arrangement cannot be reversed."

"What's that, Nikki?"

"Well, it's not Nikki anymore. As part of my going ethnic, as you call it, I have reverted to my given name - Nimrata Kaur Randhawa. Actually, the Kaur part is the surname taken by most Sikh women, based on the guidance from the 10th Sikh guru, Guru

Gobind Singh. "Kaur" is for women sort of like "Singh" is for men. So our bumper stickers and other campaign paraphernalia will read "Trump/Kaur Randhawa."

(Words fail to describe the look on Donald Trump's face as he mutters to himself: "Maybe I should have gone with Idaho senator Mike Crapo.")

I am Bolton

My name is John Bolton. I served as the National Security Advisor to President Donald J. Trump from April 2018 through September 2019. During that time, I was intimately involved with all matters affecting national security and the manner in which Donald Trump handled them. Perhaps you have read my book, "The Room Where it Happened." Perhaps not.

Because that book was intended for potentially wide public distribution, I was constrained by national security considerations in the material I could include. I was honored to be approached by the Oh Daddy Chronicles Community ("ODCC") to see if some of the classified material omitted from the book could be provided on a limited basis to the ODCC. I am pleased to report success in this regard. All of you reading this have been given Department of Energy Level Q Access Authorization (Top Secret) for a limited time. I trust you will not abuse this privilege.

In the pages that follow, I describe three matters of utmost national security sensitivity never before known outside the Oval Office: 1).The Greenland Affair, 2).The Mongolia Affair, 3).The Jakarta Affair.

The Greenland Affair

There was some media reporting in August 2019 of President Trump's interest in having the United States purchase Greenland from the country of Denmark. The reason given to the press stressed Greenland's wealth of natural resources and proximity to strategic shipping lanes.

Well, I was there for the closed door discussions between the President and Danish Prime Minister Mette Frederiksen and I can assure you those legitimate strategic interests of the United States were not even on the President's radar screen. Hell, Pompeo joked that Trump couldn't tell the difference between a shipping lane and a bowling lane even as he did his old man, too slippery for me, gingerly, mincing shuffle toward the throwing line in a bowling alley. So here's the real story.

Melania came down to breakfast one morning in the East Wing and told her husband that Barron wanted to go to the original Legoland in Billund, Denmark. And he wanted to go soon. And Donald was going to make it happen. So the President phoned the Danish Prime Minister to make arrangements. Three days later, in a return phone call, the President was informed that such a visit would not be possible for security reasons. It would be too disruptive. Furthermore, the entire summer season had been booked by a native peoples group from Greenland called "Inuits Aren't Jesuits."

That gave the President an idea which he ran by his national security team. Why not simply buy Greenland, construct a brand new super colossal Legoland Greenland in the middle of the continent, build it at super warp speed, and have Barron go there before the end of summer? That last part was the trickiest because summer in mid-continental Greenland usually lasts only a few days - and that's in even numbered years. Odd numbered years? Forget it.

Negotiations with Denmark, alas, went nowhere. The President first offered $498 billion. No deal. Then he offered the entire state of California, hoping to get rid of their electoral college votes. No way. No way the Danes could allow space cadet Elon Musk to become a Danish citizen. Out of desperation, the President offered to sign an Executive Order requiring all restaurants in the United States to offer Danish pastries as the only choice of breakfast sweet. That one almost made it, but not quite. In the end, the President's foreign policy initiative came to naught, as is usually the case.

By the way, Barron has not spoken to his father since.

The Mongolia Affair

Many conservatives are not what you would call warm and fuzzy when it comes to endangered animals. But even I, a dyed-in-the wool conservative if ever there was one, couldn't help but feel appalled by Donald Trump, Jr.'s behavior in the summer of 2019. And the repercussions just might cost American lives.

He went to Mongolia to hunt a near endangered species - a beautiful animal called the Argali sheep. He killed one. The problem was that Mongolian authorities require a rather expensive permit to kill this animal. Don Jr. had no such permit. A permit was issued retroactively 30 days later when Don Jr. was safely back in the US. No explanation was ever provided for what happened during those 30 days. Not until now.

The Mongolian President, Khaltmaagiin Battulga, demanded an apology, permit fees, and steep penalties. Our President wanted to sweep this whole thing under the rug, keeping it as quiet as possible so as not to stir up an "Argali sheep horns matter" movement. The two presidents agreed to conduct all negotiations through Ivanka Trump's personal email account, the one she had been using for government business since 2017, having been shown how to do so by Hillary Clinton's pet grooming assistant. Jared was jealous. He argued that "jdweeb@gmail.com" was less likely to draw attention. Ivanka won out.

At first, President Trump took an obstructionist negotiating tack with President Battulga, contending that nothing at all had happened. This approach went nowhere. Then he argued that the sheep didn't really die of a gunshot wound in the head, but rather from the sheep version of COVID-19. Battulga wasn't buying it because, as he so eloquently put it, "Your testing couldn't find a coronavirus in a sheep if it was throwing a New Year's Eve party on the antlers." Trump conceded the point.

By this time, our President was getting desperate. He offered to reveal to President Battulga whether Finland was actually part of Russia and whether the UK had nuclear weapons. Fortunately for Trump, his bluff was not called. Exasperated, President Trump asked his Mongolian counterpart what he wanted. Battulga demanded that Dr. Deborah Birx be sent to Mongolia to serve as Minister for Fashion and that he, Khaltmaagiin Battulga, be given country-wide franchising rights for Georgetown Cupcakes, with the right to modify cupcake offerings based on local culinary tastes, particularly yak. He asked our President what he thought of gluten- free cookies and yak cream strawberry lava fudge. Our President tactfully replied, "Yak Yuck."

President Trump agreed to President Battulga's demands and, to cement the deal, offered to send to Mongolia the first coronavirus vaccines to be produced in a sufficient quantity to vaccinate all Mongolian citizens and sheep. This forced Dr. Fauci to extend his timeline for the availability of a vaccine by about three months.

The Jakarta Affair

Little or nothing made it into the media about what became known in the Inner Circle as "The Jakarta Affair." It started innocently enough when Melania read about coffee baths in a Slovenian issue of Cosmopolitan. Bathing in coffee increased skin tone and softness. If the coffee was decaf, it helped maintain narrow, slanty, cat-like eyes, or so the article said. But not just any coffee - only coffee from coffee beans grown in a certain part of the Indonesian island of Sumatra.

So naturally, Melania wanted a shitload of those beans. After all, she was on the north side of 50 and she need only look at her husband to see what age can do to a person's looks. Problem was that she wasn't the only person to read that article. It went viral in Japan and the Japanese bought all the available beans. She insisted that the President take action. The only thing he feared more than a one-on-one lunch with Vice President Pence when the VP was in a Scripture quoting mode was Melania's wrath. So he organized a SWAT team of Kushner, Pompeo, myself, former Milwaukee police chief and certified fruitcake David Clarke, all led by the President's son Eric.

We organized an expeditionary team of Guatemalan mercenaries, with Eric leading them. Their mission was to capture, and hold by force if necessary, the largest relevant coffee bean plantations so as to secure a sufficient coffee bean supply chain from the Sumatran highlands to the decadent bathtubs of the East Wing.

The expeditionary force (10 out-of-work Guatemalan taxi drivers plus Eric Trump) landed on the southwestern shore of Sumatra, carrying keychains with a picture of Juan Valdez for good luck. The problem was that a). they were all in poor condition to climb the highlands where the coffee plantations were and b) none of them would know what a coffee plantation looked like if a coffee plant was growing out their ass. Not a recipe for success.

Anyway, they stopped about 1/3 of the way up the mountain and decided to capture the plantation in front of them. It was a betel nut plantation. Eric decided to check out the plants and soon he and the Guatemalans were stuffing betel nuts into their mouths. As you might know, betel nut is one of the most addictive drugs in the world. In short order, everyone was totally stoned. Capture was inevitable. Eric and crew were turned over to the authorities in Jakarta. The incident became known as the Bay of Lampung invasion.

Eric's identity was soon discovered and a call made to the White House. The Indonesian President - Joko Widodo - demanded that President Trump come to Jakarta in person to negotiate the release of Eric and the agreement by the Indonesians to keep the whole affair quiet.

I accompanied the President to Jakarta, but it was a struggle to get him to go. He claimed that he really preferred talking to people with two first names, like Billy Bob or Bubba John. He could even accept people with one first name. But those slippery Indonesians had a habit of using only one name in total - Sukarno, Suharto, their most famous singer Sinartro, and their most famous real estate mogul Sueallofyou. But eventually, he went to Jakarta.

After difficult negotiations, the President agreed to purchase 500 million face masks made from the traditional Indonesian black cap called a songkok. He further agreed to a national face mask requirement in the U.S. until the pandemic in the U.S. ended. President Widodo was confident of at least a few follow-on purchase orders.

Then a strange thing happened - a very strange thing. The two Presidents appeared in a televised joint news conference, following which reporters, public officials, virtually all of Indonesian society became enamored of our President. They shook his hand, took photos of his hands, wanted plaster casts of his hands, dipped his hands into bowls of holy water and drank it, danced around his hands, chanted weird sounding melodies around his hands. You get the point.

Finally, Air Force One took off for home, Eric on board. The topic of discussion turned to the obvious - what was all that hand frenzy about. An NSC staffer by the name of Hu Mi Tel, known for his extreme discretion, was also on board. Hu had a Ph.D. in comparative mythology and confidently explained what had happened. In cold northern climates, a creature known as Big Foot is an object of much speculation and fascination. In warm, tropical southern climates, such as exist in the Indonesian archipelago, the object of speculation and fascination is known as Small Hands. Accepted wisdom is that the arrival of Small Hands in the archipelago foretold great prosperity. Celebrations continued for weeks after Small Hands arrived back at the White House.

＊ ＊

There is more to tell, much more, but I might have revealed too much already.

J.B.

Tit for Tat

(The President receives a special security briefing about the Russian operation to pay Afghans to kill American soldiers. The President is outraged. When the briefing team leaves the Oval Office, he picks up the red phone on the Resolute Desk. It rings in the Kremlin.)

"Privyet, Donald. How are you today? Sorry to hear about your coronavirus mess."

"Coronavirus mess? What coronavirus mess?"

"Never mind. I just be practical jokester. What can I do for you?"

"Vladimir, I am outraged at your behavior. I never imagined you could stoop so low."

"Donald, my friend, what is problem?"

"I just learned that you have been offering $10 to Afghans for each American soldier they kill. How dare you insult the American military? A measly $10? I demand no less than $1000 per soldier."

"I did not mean to offend you, Donald. Rossian economy is heavily dependent on price of oil. Price of oil right now very low. We are on tight budget."

"I understand your predicament. How about if I get Mnuchin to arrange some financing for you on favorable terms?"

"Spasiba, Donald, thank you."

"All right, but I want you to understand how tough I will be on this if you continue with anything under $1000. You know all those Russian hot dog vendors in Manhattan?"

"Of course, my nephew Sasha runs three carts."

"Well, we have technology that can make sure the Disney song "It's a Small World After All" plays every time someone orders a hot dog - and only at the Russian carts. Pretty soon, both the customers and hot dog Dmitry won't even dream of ordering or selling a hot dog. Now, please don't force me to do this."

"Thank you for the warning, Donald. I am shaking in my Rossian Army Spetsnaz boots. But I must repay you the courtesy of advance warning. If United States forces Rossian hot dog vendors in Manhattan into bankruptcy, then we will infiltrate U.S. embassies around the world and infect with coronavirus. Then you have real problem. But I hope it does not come to this."

"I'm sure it will not. But, just in case it does, I owe it to you to give fair warning of what would happen next. I personally know the owners of the NHL teams Tampa Bay Lightning, Washington Capitals, and Pittsburgh Penguins. And I will ask them as a personal favor to demote star players Nikita Kucherov, Alex Ovechkin, and Evgeni Malkin to the minor leagues. So take that!"

"Ouch, Donald. Please no more. I shake boots so much they come off. ("Olga, since boots now off, can you massage feet?") I am impressed with your knowledge of Rossian NHL stars. I didn't know you were a hockey fan."

"I'm not. But that's all that Barron talks about these days."

"Well, I need to go, Donald. Olga finish with feet and moving up in world, as they say."

"So you agree to a minimum of $1000 per soldier if we arrange low-cost financing?"

"Da. Yes. And dasvidanya, Donald."

"Does with onion to you, too, Vladimir."

Book Worm

(At the White House press briefing on June 30, 2020, White House press secretary Kayleigh McEnany made a startling announcement.)

"The President does read."

(After the shock of this revelation wore off, people all over the country celebrated. Books arrived at the White House from all corners of the land - books, books, and more books. The President asked Secretary of Education Betsy Devos to help him sort through everything.)

"Come on in, Betsy. Looks like this is going to be another crazy day."

(Betsy Devos enters the Oval Office and takes a seat.)

"Well, sir, Kayleigh really created quite the firestorm with her remarks a few days ago. But I'm here to help you sort through everything."

(At that moment, the front doorbell of the White House rings. The White House valet opens the door.)

"Hey, look who's here - my old buddy Squishie. Que pasa, dude?"

"Hola. I'm doing fine. These Fed Ex deliveries are keeping me mucho busy. And in the evenings I've got that dancin' machine Bill Barr now coming three times a week. Damn, he's good."

"So what you got for us today?"

"These sacks of stuff - I think they're books - for old Orange Puss."

"He's in the Oval. You know how to find it."

"Sure do. Thanks. Oh, is Jared's puke receptacle still accepting donations?"

"It is. It's quite in demand, so we empty it and disinfect it every hour."

"Great. See ya dude."

(Just in front of the hallway portrait of Jared Kushner, Squishie sees his dancing protege Attorney General Bill Barr. They embrace and do all sorts of weird hand, arm, and elbow touching gestures.)

"Squish, my man, what brings you here today? Looks like you've got some heavy stuff there."

"Yep. I think it's books for old Orange Cheekbones. I been here every day this week."

"That announcement by Kayleigh took all of us by surprise. Hey. Want to get in on the pool as to which day he'll fire her?"

"Not a smokin' timber in the fox hole with a broken mirror, dude."

"Gotcha. Maybe next time. Gotta go now. See ya at the studio tomorrow."

"Right on, bro."

(Squishie enters the Oval Office, delivers the sacks of books, obtains a signature (which he later sells on eBay for $80,000), and departs.)

(Secretary DeVos reaches into the first sack.)

"The first book we have here today, Mr. President, looks like a good one. It's called "A Beginner's Guide to Racism, 1st edition." The author calls himself "Bubba." Shall I put this in the "keep" pile?"

"Yes, we'll keep it. But put it at the very bottom because I've already read the 5th edition."

"Next we have "The New Jim Crow," by Michelle Alexander. Could be useful."

"Nah. I never understood all those pansy-ass liberals who get their rocks off by standing on a wooden platform in the middle of nowhere hoping to spot some stupid bird so they can put a pin in the map on their wall. Put it in the discard pile."

"Now here's a book I'm not familiar with. Let me see. It's called Beowulf and the book jacket says it was written about 1000 years ago."

"Something to do with werewolves, maybe?"

"No idea. And there's an inscription here. Must be from the person who sent it."

"What's it say?"

"I'm coming, Grendel."

"This is really strange. We've got to find out what this is about without me reading it, even if I could."

"I'm afraid I don't know anyone who could help. Helping children actually get educated has not exactly been my focus."

"Wait. I know the perfect person to explain this to us - my buddy Matt Bevis. He's a professor of English Literature at Nabisco College at Oxford. I'll call him."

"Professor Matthew Bevis speaking. How may I help you?"

"Matt, this is your buddy Donald, as in Donald Trump, as in President of the United States. We spoke a little while ago. I've got you on the speaker phone with Betsy DeVos, our Secretary of Education."

"Ah, yes, I certainly do remember. You inquired about the word "quark" in English literature. We had a jolly good chat about James Joyce and William Shakespeare. Tell me, have you found the time to read "Dubliners" or "King Lear" yet?"

"I'm afraid not. So much cable news to watch and so little time for anything else. And now, I'm swamped with books that people all over the country have sent me once my Press Secretary blabbed to everyone that I do read."

"Yes, we did hear about that even in these hallowed halls of Keble College, Oxford."

"Keebler? I thought it was Nabisco. Anyway, here's the problem. One of the books I received is called Beowulf. And there's an inscription inside that says: "I'm coming, Grendel." Neither Secretary DeVos nor I have any idea what this is about. Can you help us?"

"I'd be delighted to. You really are in luck, old chap. Beowulf is one of the most important works of Old English literature. It is an epic poem with 3,182 alliterative lines. It's not clear when it was written, but the manuscript itself dates from 975 - 1025. The story takes place in Scandinavia in the 6th C. The protagonist, Beowulf, comes to the aid of Hrothgar, king of the Danes, whose great hall, Heorot, is plagued by the monster Grendel. Beowulf kills Grendel with his bare hands and, later, kills Grendel's mother with a giant's sword that he found in her lair."

"Interesting, but what could this book and inscription have to do with me?"

"That is a puzzlement. There was, however, a simplified American edition published about six months ago. To make it easier for the American audience, and to distinguish it from Harry Potter, Beowulf's name was changed to Joebee-won-Kenobi, or Joebee for short."

(Professor Bevis sees two colleagues in the hallway. He covers the phone and calls out: "Nigel, Clive, he got it!")

"Sorry for the interruption. So, Beowulf is the hero who rids the land of the evil Grendel and his family. I think you'll enjoy the book, old man. Is there anything else I can help you with?"

"I think not. I already have learned more than I wanted to. Thank you for your time. You can go back to your cream tea and strumpets now."

(With a quizzical, but amused, look on his face, Professor Bevis hangs up the phone.)

"This next one looks more like a collection of memoranda than an actual book. Let me see. Ahh... It's an autographed set of all the coronavirus memos Dr. Fauci has sent you since January."

(The President shuffles through the papers.)

"Doesn't look familiar at all. I guess we should keep it, but definitely bottom of the stack. Next."

"Oh. An all-time classic. Complete works of Dr. Seuss - simplified version. The Cat in the Hat, Green Eggs and Ham, How the Grinch Stole Christmas, and more."

"Betsy, don't get so excited. I haven't seen you like this since you redirected $10 million in Federal funds away from inner city schools in Chicago and sent them to Phillips Andover. Now as to this Dr. Seuss character, I have steadfastly ignored Dr. Fauci and Dr. Redfield and Dr. Hahn and usually Deborah even. Why would anyone think I would want to read what this Dr. Seuss guy has to say? Discard pile."

"Next we have the U.S. Constitution, plus a beginner's version."

"I don't need either one. I like mine better."

"Yours?"

"Yes, nice and simple. The whole Constitution in just one sentence - "The President can do whatever he wants to do." Jared made it for me on one of those make your own book websites. Even has a cover that says "Constutition" (I did that part)."

"This next one looks useful - "How to Study for the SATs, Bar Exam, and Cognitive Impairment Tests." It even includes a chapter on how to distinguish between a lion and an elephant."

"Top of the pile, Betsy. You know, I think I've had enough for now. Why don't you just read the titles of the remaining books?"

"Very well, sir. We have "Crime and Punishment" by Fyodor Dostoevsky. And it has an inscription that says "We've seen the first part; can't wait for the last part." Then there's "How to Totally Screw Up a Country in Less Than Four Years, for Dummies." We have "League of American Traitors" by Matthew Landis, "Everyone Poops," by Taro Gomi, "How to Win Friends and Influence People," by Dale Carnegie, and "Manners Can be Fun," by Munroe Leaf... Wait. There's one more. Ah, an American classic - "Of Mice and Shitheads" - by John Steinbeck."

"Steinbeck? We've got of those in the White House grand ballroom. We let Barron take his piano lessons on it."

"I guess that's it for today, sir. Anything else?"

"Actually, yes. I don't want any more of these damn books. Tell Kayleigh that because she created the problem, she has to fix it."

(Secretary DeVos leaves. Two days later, White House Press Secretary Kayleigh McEnany holds another briefing.)

"The President is extremely grateful for the overwhelming response to the revelation I made in the June 30 briefing that "The President does read." He has received an untold number of books from patriotic Americans all over the country. However, I must kindly ask that no more books be sent. You see, once again, the Fake News media such as you all gathered here now misinterpreted my statement. "Read" clearly means to take in information from a book.

The President does that. But he does it with his ears, not his eyes. His "reading" is solely from audio books. So again, thank you to all the hard-working, brave, mostly white American people who sent a book, but enough is enough. All books that have been received will be donated to Saint Andrew's Episcopal School, which is the school the President's son Barron attends."

EPISODE XXXI

Damn Yankees

(Chief of Staff Mark Meadows enters the Oval Office.)

"Come on in, Mark. Have a seat."

(The President is throwing rolled up wads of paper towards the trash can in the corner. The trash can exhibits no signs of fear, for obvious reasons.)

"Mark, we have a problem. Everyone is making such a big deal about Fauci's throwing out the first pitch at that baseball game. They even have a baseball card for him and his mask. It's their all-time bestseller. We've got to top that."

"Maybe you could throw out the first pitch at Yankee Stadium."

"I already tried that. They said no. So I announced I would do it anyway and then cancelled."

"That was clever thinking on your part, sir. But maybe next time you could pay the Yankees a few million dollars to back up your story. And also maybe send the acceptance tweet before the cancellation tweet."

"Good thinking, but that doesn't solve our problem. You need to find me some events for which I can get the ball rolling."

"I'll get right on it, sir."

(Several days later, the Chief of Staff returns to the Oval Office.)

"I think I've found some great events for you to kick off, sir. But first, do you want me to look into why the maid hasn't been cleaning the Oval Office?"

"What do you mean, Mark?"

"Well, sir, there's that mountain of rolled up wads of paper in the corner. You can hardly see the trash can."

"The maid comes in twice a day. That pile is all from this morning. So what do you have lined up for me?"

"The first one is the Naki Sumo Baby Crying Competition at the Sensoji Temple in Japan. Every year, people gather to see sumo wrestlers climb into a ring, each one carrying a baby. The sumo wrestlers try to make the babies cry and the baby that cries the most is declared the winner, along with its sumo wrestler."

"Hmm... So you think I would be better than sumo wrestlers at making babies cry?"

"What? Oh, no sir. I was thinking you would be one of the crying babies inasmuch as you have so much practice at it."

"What's next?"

"I've already booked you as an honored guest participant in the World Worm Charming Championships in Willaston - a small village in England. Participant groups of three are each given a square meter patch of ground from which they must coax as many worms as possible to come to the surface."

"You're kidding right?"

"Not at all, sir. This is legit. And given your experience of worming your way out of the woodwork to disgust people, I figured you'd be a natural. The betting line already has your group as the favorite."

"Is that all, Mark?"

"No way, sir. I've been hard at work. Next you're going to Sonkajärvi in Finland."

"Now this sounds good. Since Finland is part of Russia, I'm guessing Vladimir will be there to greet me."

"Uh, actually, sir, Finland became independent of Russia on December 6, 1917. But not to worry. You'll be participating in Eukokanto - the World Wife Carrying Championships. You run an obstacle course carrying a woman weighing at least 108 pounds, with the woman slung over your shoulder like a sack of potatoes."

"I'm not so sure about this one. Melania's been eating a lot of twinkies lately. Does it have to be the carrier's wife?"

"No, sir. It can be any woman who meets the weight requirement."

"I've got it. I'll get Pelosi to be my partner, in a true spirit of working together. Then when I get to the running through the mud part, I'll conveniently lose my grip and down she splatters. Make sure the camera crews are ready."

"Sounds like a plan, sir. Are you up for one more?"

"Just one, Mark. Just one."

"This one should be a bit easier, sir. The Cooper's Hill Cheese Rolling Competition in Gloucestershire, England has invited you to be the master of ceremonies at their next annual competition. The event involves the master of ceremonies releasing a nine-pound wheel of Double Gloucester cheese, which rolls down a hill at a speed of 70 miles per hour. Participants run after it, trying to be the first to reach the cheese at the bottom of the hill."

"Sounds like fun. But why have they invited me in particular?"

"They said they were struck by the remarkable similarity between the color of their orange hued Double Gloucester cheese and that of the Presidential visage."

"You've done a great job, Mark. This stuff will really piss off Fauci. Eat your heart out, Mr. Popularity!"

(Chief of Staff Meadows leaves to make travel arrangements.)

Donald and the Beanstalk

(The Oval Office secretary announces the arrival of Mr. Robert Unanue, CEO of Goya Foods.)

"Come on in, Bob. It's great to have you here. Sycophants like you are always welcome."

"Thank you, Mr. President. You know, we have a lot in common. Both of us got to lead large businesses and become very wealthy due to the hard work of ancestors. For you, your father. For me, my grandfather. You might know the Goya story, but I would like to state it briefly if I may."

"Certainly. And feel free to spice it up." (The President chortles at his cleverness.)

"Goya Foods was founded in 1936 in New York City by Spanish immigrants - my grandfather Don Prudencio Unanue and his wife Carolina. Since then, the company has become the largest Hispanic owned food company in the United States and the premier source for authentic Latin cuisine."

"Very impressive, Bob, but where does the name Goya come from?"

"It comes from the 18th and early 19th Century Spanish painter Francisco Goya. We consider our products to be works of art."

"Fascinating. Who would have thought to name a company after some dead Spanish guy who went around painting houses?

Not me, certainly. And I had the opportunity, you know. One of the dead guys in my family tree started out as a house painter in Austria. I've always looked up to him. But anyway, let's get down to business. What's on your mind?"

"Well, you know that the boycott of Goya products - the one that began when I licked your ass in public - has been going on for a while now. Hell, I was just practicing my Mike Pence impersonation. Anyway, the boycott has been having a very negative effect on our business. We were forced to explore other avenues to promote our products."

"Any luck?"

"Yes, and this is where you come in. Win-win situation big time for both of us. Want the details?"

"Of course. Spill the beans." (President again chortles at his mastery of the English language.)

"We did some cross breeding genetic modification research at our super-secret cultivation testing location in the remote Bolivian highlands. The results stunned us. We were able to grow a type of black bean with a most unusual property. If the consumer of the beans was a Democrat, the beans converted him or her into a Republican. If the consumer of the beans was a Republican, there was no change."

"That's amazing and, obviously, potentially extremely useful. How long does the effect last?"

"More research needs to be done, but preliminary results suggest immunity from being a Democrat lasts about one year. Booster bean intake strengthens the effect."

"Wow. So what do you propose?"

"We both benefit from widespread consumption of these beans. But I need marketing help right now. My idea is that you spearhead an all-of-government response to foist these beans on unwitting consumers. Then you get re-elected and I get richer. What do you say?"

"I say let's go for it. All out. But I have to be careful pushing the plan to Ivanka and Jared."

"Why? I thought they were your most trusted go-to sleazeballs?"

"They are. Cream of the sleazeball crop. But they're both Jewish and might be skeptical of a plan hatched by a Goya. But I'm sure I'll be able to bring them around."

"Great, but we need to discuss one possible problem with the supply chain."

"OK. What is it? My Administration has had great success with supply chains so we'll deal with it, whatever it is."

"These magic beans, grown in the soil of the Bolivian highlands, lose their potency if transported the distance from Bolivia to the United States. We need to have them grown right here in the U.S."

"That should be no problem. I'll have Secretary of Agriculture Frank Perdue get right on it."

"Well, it's not that simple, sir. These beans are very particular about where they can grow. Our research clearly shows that the only place in the U.S. suitable for them is right here in the White House Rose Garden. So we need to convert the Rose Garden into a Bean Garden. Can it be done?"

"Of course it can. I'll have press secretary Kayleigh McEnany announce that the White House chef needed a kitchen bean garden. Kayleigh has a lot of practice saying ridiculous things with a straight face. So problem solved. Let's move on this."

"Excellent, sir. I'll have my people get the seeds to Secretary Perdue. And I've even come up with a marketing slogan - "Black Beans Matter.""

(The President cringes.)

"Think about it, sir. Our target demographics on this one is not your base, it's the other 90% of the country."

"I guess you have a point, Bob. Let's keep in touch on this."

(Robert Unanue leaves the Oval Office.)

(A few hours later, Secretary of Agriculture Sonny Perdue enters the Oval Office. The President is arranging and rearranging cans of Goya black beans on the Resolute Desk. He is thinking of enlisting the services of his OCD Vice President to get the arrangement just right.)

"You asked to see me, sir. But might I be permitted to recommend that the can of beans second on the right needs to be moved 2.4 centimeters to the left?"

"Really? You think so? Hell, the Fake News types probably think I should get a scientific opinion from Fauci. But I'm throwing caution to the wind. Consider it moved. And who needs Pence anyway?"

"Much better, sir. Now, what is it that you wished to discuss with me?"

"Here's the deal, Frank. And this is going to be even more important than a tough man like yourself making a tender chicken."

"Excuse me, sir. I think you are confusing me with Frank Perdue. He was the CEO of Perdue Farms and used the marketing slogan "It takes a tough man to make a tender chicken." Frank Perdue died in 2005. I am Sonny Perdue, former two term governor of the state of Georgia. I don't know shit about chickens."

"That's OK because this has nothing to do with chickens, it's all about beans. I have a top secret project - demanding a whole-of-government response - that I need you to lead."

(The President explains what he and Robert Unanue discussed.)

"Do you think you can handle it, Sonny?"

"No problem, sir. This is going to be a blast. I love beans."

(A major marketing blitz is rolled out over the next few weeks. Here are some of the highlights.)

Treasury Secretary Mnuchin - "Bargain price beans. Makes your inadequate stimulus check go further."

Secretary of State Pompeo - "I've traveled the globe to find the best beans. And here they are - literally in my backyard."

Defense Secretary Esper - "Goya black beans definitely dominate the beanspace."

Attorney General William Barr - "The Justice Department certifies that these Spanish beans have entered the country legally. All others will be deported."

Melania Trump - "If you can't find Slovenian beans, zen zese beans are ze next best choice."

White House Federal Express delivery man Squishie - "Now these are some mighty badass beans!"

Assistant to the President Peter Navarro - "Everyone who orders three or more cans of Goya beans will receive my 500 page eBook - "Fart Your Way to Freedom."

Coronavirus Task Force Response Coordinator Dr. Deborah Birx - "I can say with confidence that there are no documented cases of coronavirus transmission involving Goya beans. I cannot make the same assertion with respect to other brands. Act accordingly."

Coronavirus testing czar Admiral Brett Giroir - "As Dr. Birx has stated, we believe that Goya beans are quite safe with respect to coronavirus. Nevertheless, out of an abundance of caution, in my role as coronavirus testing czar, I have arranged for dedicated bean testing sites to be set up around the country. If you have any reason to suspect that one of your beans might be coronavirus positive, get it tested at no cost to you. And don't worry about using up valuable reagents and transport media, we use that scuzzy disgusting bean stuff in the can for those purposes."

Ivanka Trump - "As delicious as they are cute."

Donald Trump - "Powerful beans make powerful farts. Take it from me."

(One month into the Goya magic black beans campaign, sales are going through the roof. Expecting a similar effect on his poll numbers, the President calls his new campaign manager, Bill Stepien, into the Oval Office. The President can hardly contain his expectant glee.)

"So Bill, tell me the good news about our poll numbers."

"Well, Mr. President, I'm afraid I don't have any. Your poll numbers are decreasing faster than coronavirus cases are increasing. And it's not due to increased sample sizes in the polling. Your negativity rates are astonishing. You've got the lowest poll numbers of any presidential candidate in history at this stage of the race. We don't know what to attribute it to or how to reverse it."

"WTF? Get out of here, Bill. And, by the way, you're fired."

(Just then, the Oval Office secretary announces that Mr. Robert Unanue is in the waiting area and seems quite agitated. He is admitted to the Oval Office.)

"Bob, what the fuck is going on? Sales are way up but my poll numbers are way down. Even in Idaho! Explain!"

"That's why I rushed over to see you, sir. You need to understand that magic black bean development designed to immunize a person politically in a specified way is very difficult work and usually requires several years. Because of the immediacy we faced with the election in November, we were forced to proceed at warp speed. While we were as careful as possible, it turns out that there is one attribute of this novel black bean that no one anticipated. It was a complete surprise. Totally unforeseen."

"And what is this attribute?"

"The bean was developed in Bolivian soil which is in the southern hemisphere. And it was clearly demonstrated to turn Democrats into Republicans, while leaving Republicans unchanged. But when the bean was grown in the northern hemisphere - specifically the Bean Garden in the White House - it made a hemispheric shift, turning Republicans into Democrats. Who would have thought?"

"Shit! What can we do? Is there a way to reverse the effect?"

"I'm afraid not, sir. Once this bean is in the gastrointestinal tract of its host, it's there to stay. At least for one year. I would say, sir, that your re-election chances now don't amount to a hill of beans."

(Robert Unanue exits, leaving the President slumped in his chair, head in his hands.)

EPISODE XXXIII

Sverige

(Dr. Scott Atlas, the President's newest pandemic advisor, enters the Oval Office.)

"Have a seat, Scott. What's on your mind?"

"Well, Mr. President, I think we should pursue the Swedish model."

"Swedish model? Nah. It won't work."

"What makes you say that, sir? Have you been talking to Fauci recently?"

"Fauci? I haven't spoken to Fauci in months. Nothing to discuss with him."

"Then why are you so convinced we shouldn't pursue the Swedish model?"

"I already tried it - twice in fact. Didn't even get to first base with either Scarlett Johansson or Tiger Woods's ex-wife. Zippo."

"Uh... I had a different Swedish model in mind. And besides, Scarlett Johansson is American with a Jewish mother and a Danish father."

"Really? Well, I'm game for another try. Just don't tell Melania."

"I'm thinking of the Swedish model for the coronavirus."

"Great idea. Turns me on when they get breathless."

"I'm afraid I'm not making myself clear, sir. There is an alternative strategy for dealing with the coronavirus. Only a few countries have followed it, with Sweden being the highest profile country to try it. So it has become known as the "Swedish model."

"And how does this strategy differ from the strategy we've followed in the U.S.?"

"I really don't know, sir."

"What? How can you push this Swedish strategy and not know what it is?"

"I know the Swedish strategy quite well, but I have no idea what, if anything, has been the U.S strategy."

"Good point."

"The Swedish model is also known as the pursuit of herd immunity. Basically, you want pretty much everyone to get the virus and hope that only Democrats die. Open economy. Open schools. No masks. Lots of political rallies."

"Hmm. I'm liking what I hear. If we adopt this Swedish model, and I send military attack helicopters into the liberal Democrat controlled cities to stop Antifa terrorists, will the choppers blast "Dancing Queen" and "Take a Chance on Me" as they swoop down?"

"I'm sure it can be arranged, sir."

"You know, if we do this, I'd be doing a big favor for Sweden. But I'd like them to do me a favor, though. Many of the Trump Organization properties are badly in need of new furniture. Can someone arrange for us to get a 30% discount at IKEA?"

"I'm sure it can arranged, sir."

"If we go down this path, how many people are likely to die?"

"Hard to say, sir, but most models put the figure at around 2 million."

"Can we say it'll be 4 million? Then if we end up at 2 million, I can claim that I saved 2 million lives."

"Good thinking, sir. But for full and fair disclosure, I must alert you to some potential negatives about this approach."

"Such as?"

"This approach encourages people to vote in person. Seems to me that it's harder to steal a Democrat person than it is to steal a Democrat mail-in ballot. And then there's the Sanders issue."

"As in Bug-eyed Bernie Sanders?"

"Yes, sir. You know how Sanders is always saying how this country should be more like Denmark? Well, what if he decides that Sweden is close enough and gives full support to this approach? Then you would be tarnished by association with him and your base might get pissed."

"I think I can handle them. Anything else important about this Sweden approach I need to consider?"

"Well, do you like hard bread that will break your teeth? How about mini-sized meatballs? And be prepared for every dessert to contain lingonberries, even though they're more sour than your puss. And, oh yes, people in the U.S. will have to follow the example of Swedes and drink their milk in the store."

"Why do Swedes do that?"

"Because on the milk carton it says "oppnas har."

"And that means?"

"Open here."

"OK. I'm convinced. Tell Pence to get it going. No, wait. Tell Pence that I order him to pursue the best Swedish model. That'll put him in a tizzy. And report back to me in two weeks."

"Will do, sir."

(Two weeks later. Dr. Anthony Fauci enters the Oval Office.)

"Tony, what are you doing here? Dr. Atlas is supposed to brief me."

"I know. But Dr. Atlas is unable to do so, sir. He's on a ventilator."

Between the Slices

(Don Jr. and his brother Eric enter the Oval Office.)

"Boys, boys, boys. Always good to see you. Tell me what mischief you've been up to lately."

(Don Jr. does the talking.)

"Not much, dad. We've been preoccupied. Things are not going so well."

"What is it? Don't tell me your girlfriend Kimberly Tinfoyle hasn't recovered yet from the COVID-19 she got at Mt. Rushmore. How is she, anyway?"

"She's fine now, dad. No, it's something else. Eric and I have been going through the financial reports for the Trump Organization properties and we are in deep trouble."

"How deep?"

"Deep spelled with four "e"s.

"Isn't that the normal way?"

"Dad. Something has to be done. Luckily, Eric and I have a plan, but we might need your help."

"OK, but I have always spelled "Deeeep State" with four "e"s. What's the plan?"

"You know that the hottest selling lunch item - and sometimes also at dinner - at many of our properties is a grilled cheese sandwich."

"I love a grilled cheese sandwich. By the way, how many "e"s does cheese have?"

"Dad, you need to focus. We were thinking. What if we could continue to serve grilled cheese sandwiches, at the normal grilled cheese sandwich price, but prepare them without the cheese? Our costs would go down, profit margins per sandwich would go up, and we might be able to stave off bankruptcy. Of course, the problem is that no one knows how to make a grilled cheese sandwich without the cheese that tastes the same as one with the cheese."

"Good point. So..."

"So we put together a top secret research project to figure out how to do this. We've even located the scientist to spearhead the efforts - a guy named Herr Doctor Professor Ignatius Cheese from the University of Heidelberg, just recently relocated there from Paraguay. What do you think?"

"Well, I've heard of wackier ideas."

"Like injecting a person with disinfectant to kill the coronavirus?"

"Yeah. I guess that one's wackier. But who are you going to test this out on, assuming Dr. Cheese comes up with a recipe?"

"We don't know. We were hoping you could figure something out on that end. What do you think?"

"I've got just the guy for this. You boys scoot off and let me get to work."

"Bye, pops."

(Don Jr. and Eric leave the Oval Office. Attorney General William Barr enters a few minutes later and boogies his way into his usual chair.)

"Good morning, Bill. Please sit down. I've got a project for you."

"Good morning, Mr. President. Before we start, would you like to see the new dance move I learned from Squishie last night?"

"In a word, No!"

"So what's this new project? I hope it doesn't involve overnight travel this weekend because Squishie and I are performing a boogie boys pas de deux on Saturday at the Ultra Bar on F Street."

"Probably no travel involved, but you might have to be on stand-by if something goes wrong. Here's the problem. I need to gather up a few hundred people for a secret experiment in a secret location and no one can be allowed to know that the government is behind it all. And we don't want to have to pay them. Any ideas?"

"Hmm. Let me ponder... Yes, I've got it. We send Federal law enforcement officers, dressed in camouflage uniforms to conceal their identities, into the Democrat controlled cities where the low-life anarchist types are protesting. Our stormtroopers kidnap a few hundred protestors, blindfold them, bundle them into unmarked vans without social distancing, and whisk them away to the top secret experiment location. Problem solved."

"But what if the protestors we nab don't like grilled cheese sandwiches?"

"Huh? Grilled cheese sandwiches?"

"Oh, that was supposed to be a secret. I'm afraid I'll have to shoot you now, Bill."

(Barr turns a whiter shade of pale.)

"Just kidding. But I can't reveal any more. The protestors we take can't be grilled cheese sandwich haters."

"No problem. We load some choppers with grilled cheese sandwiches and airdrop them into the crowd. Drones take photos of everything and identify anyone who chows down and seems to enjoy it. The Artificial Intelligence loaded drones then squirt indelible mustard onto their faces, allowing our camouflaged agents easy identification of who to kidnap."

"Wow. We have the technology to do that?"

"Well, you'd be surprised what a $6 billion budget for black food ops can get you. It was all Esper's idea once you got rid of Mattis."

"Perfect, Bill. I knew I could count on you. Make it happen. Don Jr. will coordinate details with you. And, by the way, if I ever see you boogying in this room again, you're fired."

(The Attorney General leaves the Oval Office.)

(A week later Attorney General Barr returns to the Oval Office to update the President on the status of the recruitment of test subjects.)

"I'm pleased to report, Mr. President, that we have now gathered our full complement of 300 grilled cheese loving test subjects."

"Super. Who did you pick up?"

"It was quite a variety of law-breaking low-lifes. There was a bunch of 8 year-old girls with pigtails who were drawing a hopscotch outline on a public sidewalk, using pink chalk no less. We got a love-struck Generation Z couple carving a heart into an oak tree in a public park. We nailed about 15 people, including some grannies, for jaywalking after we unleashed our killer chihuahuas on them. The list goes on, but I won't bore you with it."

"Excellent work, Bill. I think your involvement in this is now complete. Remember, not a word to anyone."

"Yes, sir. My lips are sealed, except when I eat that grilled cheese sandwich."

(The Attorney General departs.)

(The scene shifts to a large, previously unused cow manure storage facility in eastern Oregon. Approximately 300 "protestors" are gathered in the middle of the facility. Dr. Cheese addresses them from an elevated mezzanine level behind protective glass and sitting at a large console.)

"Velcome my dear guinea pigs. I am called Herr Doctor Professor Ignatius Cheese. I vill be guiding you through zis important experiment, ja? You vill follow my instructions or you vill die.

"For ze next two veeks, you vill be eating more grilled cheese sandviches zan you have ever eaten in your miserable lives. And you vill be eating zem while blindfolded. You vill have cheddar, brie, monterey jack, bleu, mozzarella, gruyere, feta, gouda. You vill write down your opinion of each sandvich using a scale of 1-10. Ja?"

(The experiment continues for the next two weeks, without favorable results. Dr. Cheese confers with his lead assistant.)

"I do not understand vhy ve cannot figure zis out. Ve have tried everysing."

"But I don't think you have tried Swiss. Maybe we should?"

"You really sink zere is a hole in my theory? OK, let's try."

(After one more week, they met with success. Removing cheddar from the sandwich, leaving only the bread slices, did not work. Likewise, removing brie or gouda or gruyere or any of the other cheeses. But, finally, when they combined gouda and Swiss, and then removed the combination, leaving only the bread slices, they had found the magic recipe.)

(Two weeks later. Don Jr. and Eric return to the Oval Office.)

"Come in, boys, and give me the good news. Does everyone like the new grilled cheese sandwich?"

"Actually, they did. Dr. Cheese came through on that score."

"Why do you say "did"? Not anymore?"

"We honestly don't know if everyone still likes them."

"Why not?"

"Because all of the Trump Organization properties have been shut down until further notice by local health authorities. Dr. Cheese forgot to tell us that the cheese removed from the grilled cheese sandwiches had to be pasteurized. Everyone got salmonella poisoning."

Cast in Stone

(Senator John Hoeven enters the Oval Office.)

"Come in and have a seat. I forget your name but that's not important. Can you help me with my Mt. Rushmore project?"

"I'm sorry, sir, but I have no knowledge of such a project. And besides, I am the senior senator from North Dakota. Mt. Rushmore is not in my state."

"Oh. Then you can leave now."

(A bit later, Senator Ben Sasse enters the Oval Office.)

"Even though I hate you, I want your help with my Mt. Rushmore project."

"I'm sorry, King Donnie, but you're talking gibberish again. I neither know of such a project nor would I be able to locate a Mt. Rushmore in my state of Nebraska. Sounds like more unconstitutional slop. I'm outta here."

(He leaves.)

(The President calls Kellyanne Conway into the Oval Office.)

"Kellyanne, I'm having some problems with my Mt. Rushmore project."

"I'll help in any way I can, Mr. President."

"First of all, where the hell is Mt. Rushmore?"

"Why, I believe it's in the same place it's always been. And the carvings are in the same place they've been in since Gutzon Borglum and his son Lincoln finished them in 1941."

"No, Kellyanne, I want to know the state the carvings are in."

"Well, I'll check with the Department of the Interior for confirmation, but I'm pretty sure they're in a very good state - pretty much like new. Mint condition."

"No, no, no. What state of the United States is Mt. Rushmore located in?"

"Ah, sorry. Mt. Rushmore is in South Dakota, in the Black Hills to be specific."

"Thank you. Jared has done a lot of work looking into the technical details of getting my face up there on Mt. Rushmore, but I'm having a problem with permits. I'd like you to put some pressure on the South Dakota senators about this."

"What about the governor of South Dakota - Kristi Noem?"

"No luck there. I've already tried. Even tried to bribe her with the Vice Presidency if she could pull it off."

"I'm afraid our hands are tied, Mr. President. The Black Hills arguably belong to the Lakota Sioux Native Americans. They consider the mountain to be sacred and the carvings to be a desecration. And especially with the recent increase in awareness of social injustice, the BHM movement has gathered momentum."

"BHM movement?"

"Black Hills Matter."

"Damn. I don't know who else to try."

"What about Tom Daschle?"

"Daschle. Wait. That name rings a bell... I remember. Wasn't he the next door neighbor of that troublemaker who goes around calling himself the Chronicler-in-Chief of the Oh Daddy Chronicles for the year he lived in DC?"

"Indeed, sir, and Daschle also served as Majority Leader of the United States Senate for a few years."

"But he was a Democrat and an Obama supporter, so forget him. I guess I'll just have to tell Jared that all his work was in vain. Thank you, Kellyanne."

(Kellyanne leaves the Oval Office.)

(A few hours later, the President summons Jared Kushner to the Oval Office.)

"Come in, my boy. I'm afraid I have disappointing news. The Mt. Rushmore project is not going to happen. All that work you and your team put into it was for naught."

(Jared speaks when his sobbing finally subsides.)

"We did such great, innovative, high tech work! As you know, the initial problem was when we were told that no rock could be found that was thick enough to match your head. My high tech buddies from Silicon Valley found a workaround with GPS guided high-powered explosives that could blast into the rock face simultaneously, creating the carving in a matter of seconds. We even conducted a successful proof-of-concept test."

"You mean the explosion I ordered in Beirut? Then cleverly claimed it was a terrorist attack to divert attention?"

"That's the one. Although one could argue it was, indeed, a terrorist attack. And I must say that, although I still believe my father has no equal in the criminal world, you come a close second."

"Thank you, my boy. But we just have to let this one go."

(Kellyanne Conway races into the Oval Office, waving a sheaf of papers.)

"Great news! Great news! The Nabisco Company has just agreed to imprint an outline of your hair on the downward facing side of the creme filling in Oreo cookies."

EPISODE XXXVI

Neither Snow Nor Rain...

(New Postmaster General Louis DeJoy enters the Oval Office.)

"I've gone over your proposal for a thorough revamping of the U.S. Postal Service and I must say I'm impressed. It's just what we need to handle things for November."

"I'm glad you approve, Mr. President. I'll get right on the implementation."

"If you don't mind, Killjoy, I would like to make the hiring decisions myself, with your help of course."

"No problem, sir. I'll get the ball rolling."

(One week later, Lovejoy enters the Oval Office for the first hiring decision.)

"Have a seat, Joystick. I'll conduct the interview. OK, let's see. Your teeth look fine, your feet are in good shape. Hair is brushed nicely. And your coat should do you well in cold weather. You're hired. Joy Dishwashing Liquid, order 10,000."

"Will do, sir."

(The following Tuesday, the Postmaster General returns with another difficult decision for the President to make.)

"Alright. Let's examine. Nice, sturdy body. Sharp looking wheels. Roomy interior. I could go with a slightly darker color, though, for the finish. Order 5,000."

"Done, sir."

"What about fuel, Shit Joy? Will we have enough?"

"Absolutely, sir. All you have to do is invoke the Defense Production Act and put those out-of-work farmers back to work. They'll love you for it."

"Great idea. Let's roll this out."

(The major overhaul of the U.S. Postal Service is put into operation. Oh What Joy returns to the Oval Office to debrief the President.)

"I'm not sure I like the look on your face. Has there been a problem?"

"Well, all the purchasing and hiring decisions you made were excellent."

"So then what's the problem?"

"There was just one thing we overlooked."

"And that is?"

"We forgot to hire an army of street cleaners. People everywhere are complaining about stepping in it."

"Shit."

"Exactly, sir."

Pass the Fruitcake

(Dr. Stella Gwandiku-Ambe Immanuel enters the Oval Office.)

"Dr. Immanuel. So nice to finally meet you. I am a big fan of yours. Please have a seat."

"Thank you, Mr. President. It is an honor to be here. And thank you for retweeting my video. Demon sex is a public health concern that has not gotten enough attention."

"I couldn't agree more. But first, can you tell me something about your background?"

"Certainly. I grew up in Cameroon."

"In what city? Toronto maybe?"

"No, sir. Toronto is in Canada. I am from Cameroon. That is a country in Central Africa. I got my medical education at the University of Calabar in Nigeria. That is also not in Canada. It, too, is in Central Africa, just north of Cameroon. I later came to the United States. I have a private medical practice in a strip mall in Houston, right next to my Firepower Ministries church."

"Very impressive. Now tell me about some of your medical insights, if you would, especially as they relate to COVID-19."

"Of course. There is no reason for people to wear masks. We have a magical cure - hydroxychloroquine. In my country, malaria is a big problem. Everyone take hydroxychloroquine. In all my medical experience in Cameroon and Nigeria over the past 20 years, no one ever get COVID-19 after taking hydroxychloroquine. I think your Mr. Navarro said it best - "It works."

"Your conclusion on this is obviously based on strong scientific evidence based on your experience in Africa. Impressive."

"Well, sir, my conclusion actually is based on evidence even more reliable - Reggie."

"Reggie? Who is Reggie?"

"Reggie? He my medicinal snake I bring from Cameroon."

"So how does Reggie fit in here?"

"If I want to know if a particular medicine is good or not, I hold it in front of Reggie's face. If he sticks out his tongue and touches the medicine, that is scientific proof the medicine works. Never fail. When I hold hydroxychloroquine, together with picture of coronavirus, in front of Reggie, he swallow both. Of course, he had not eaten since he found that pig in the backyard three days before. Whatever."

"Amazing, but please don't tell that story to Melania. Her Uncle Slobodan, the pig farmer from Zagorje ob Savi, is quite sensitive to that sort of thing. I hear that you have some other interesting theories. Tell me about them."

"Well, they not theories, Mr. President. They scientific fact. First is demon sex and I don't mean what that weird Jew Elian Muskovitz does with the Mrs."

"So what demon sex are you talking about if not that one?"

"I talk about when a demon visits a woman when she is sleeping and they have sex in her dreams. This often results in gynecological problems like cysts and endometriosis. Can be very painful. I interview many women with these problems and almost all say they cannot remember having sex with a demon in their dreams."

"So how does that prove your theory?"

"Well, demons very clever, as you should know. They make women forget their dreams. And besides, Reggie agree."

"What treatment do you offer for these situations?"

"Hydroxychloroquine, of course."

"Of course. Oh dopey me. What other insights can you share?"

"Well, as you know Mr. President, being the smart man you are, alien DNA is currently being used in medical treatment."

"To what end?"

"At first, it was just the routine use - treating ingrown toenails and tennis elbow. But now they are experimenting with human cloning, trying to create a Democratic National Alien (DNA) so as to rig the upcoming election."

"Oh shit! I'll have to issue an immediate Executive Order demanding that all research involving DNA be halted and funds shifted to RNA research. Anything else in that big bosom, sorry, I mean brain of yours?"

"Yessir. I know you are very proud of the coronavirus vaccine research going on, but you should be more than a little bit careful. There is vaccine research underway that would prevent people from being religious. At first, the elites just called that vaccine "education," but now that Secretary DeVos has had her way for the last 3 1/2 years, they think something more drastic is needed.

"And there is one more thing you should know, Mr. President. Reptilians have infiltrated the government and are taking over. You call them the Deep State, but they are actually reptilian hemorrhoids, and can be a real pain in the ass."

"How can I know if someone in my government is actually a Deep State Reptilian?"

"Give the person in question hydroxychloroquine. If they start to look like Dr. Fauci wearing a scarf, then you know."

"This has all been very interesting, Dr. Immanuel, but there is a reason I asked you here that I haven't yet told you about. You see, I have a problem - a problem with my coronavirus task force. "A few days ago, Dr. Redfield got his chin fungus caught in a high-speed blender. The facial reconstruction surgery will put him out of commission for two months. When Dr. Birx ran over to help Redfield, her scarf got caught in the darn machine and they still haven't been able to get it out. They extracted her, but she faces the same two month recovery from facial and neck reconstruction surgery. I visited her in the hospital yesterday. Her neck still looks like something that would make Mitch McConnell drool with envy. She's also undergoing counseling, trying to come to terms with the possibility of never being able to wear a scarf again. Then there's Dr. Hahn. He's suffering severe adverse effects of that new hair growing drug he rushed through his own FDA. And finally, none other than Mr. Everyone's Favorite Person, Dr. Fauci. He quit and signed a two-year contract with the Washington Nationals as their new mascot, also getting a 20% cut of hot dog vendor revenues once fans return.

"So I have no doctors left on the coronavirus task force. I was hoping that you would agree to join the task force as lead medical member. And, as a bonus, you and Pence can discuss all that God and Jesus stuff. What do you say?"

"I am more than honored, Mr. President. But are you sure I am the right person for the position?"

"Absolutely. You've got everything I'm looking for. You agree with me on hydroxychloroquine and masks. Your ideas are so nutty they make even my most absurd ones look almost sane. Your accent makes you even harder to understand than does my idiotic syntax. And there's no way your ratings and popularity can be higher than mine. You're perfect."

"Well then, I accept, Mr. President. I'll just gather up my things in Houston - Reggie, my ouija board which I use as point-of-care testing; and my hat collection. By the way, do you think Dr. Birx would lend me her scarf collection now that she's not using it? That way, maybe no one would notice that she's been replaced."

(Dr. Immanuel leaves the Oval Office. The President has a satisfied look on his face as he stalks around the Oval Office pointing with the Reptilian Deep State divining rod he ordered from Amazon Prime.)

EPISODE XXXVIII

TikTok

(In the White House briefing room, Kayleigh McEnany opens the press briefing with an unexpected announcement.)

"Good afternoon. Contrary to what all of you have reported, the President has no intention of banning the Chinese social media platform TikTok from operating in the United States. In fact, he has never had any such intentions. Once again, the Fake News has gotten the story all wrong."

(Reporter): "So there is no TikTok ban?"

"Did I say there is no tic tock ban? No, I didn't say that. Why don't you listen to what I say, for a change? The President's ability to concentrate on his ball swinging thingy in the Oval Office has been seriously impaired by the large grandfather clock there and its loud "tic tock" noise. Therefore, he has banned this "tic tock" from the Oval Office. He has also banned the use of "Tic Tac" candy from the Oval Office. Too many people were spitting out the new flavor and denting his ball swinging thingy. I hope that clears things up."

(Flashback to three days prior to Kayleigh's announcement.)

(The door to the Oval Office swings open and in walks Barron William Trump, 14 year-old son of Donald and Melania Trump.)

"Well, look who it is. Sit down, son. How long has it been?"

"Mom says it's been about eight years."

"Eight years? No way it's been that long since I've seen you."

"What? Oh, sorry. I thought you were talking about the last time you and mom had sex."

"So the new school year is starting. Are you disappointed that it will only be distance learning?"

"Yeah, kind of. I'll miss seeing my friends every day, but I can still stay in close contact with Percival Osbourne."

"Percival Osbourne? Is he your best friend?"

"Oh, no. He kind of really hates me, but he's by far the smartest kid in the school."

"So why do you need to stay in close contact with him?"

"I have him on retainer to take the SATs for me in a couple of years."

"Ah. Good forward planning. Will you be getting more home-work assignments this year?"

"That's what we've been told. A lot more. But I have things under control. Aunt Maryanne has agreed to do a lot of it for me. She says she has a lot of experience in this area."

"So what do you like to do in your spare time?"

"I'm really into K-Pop."

"Really? Your mother now has this thing for twinkies and you're into that cake stuff that looks like a lollipop."

"Those are cake pops, dad. I'm talking about K-Pop."

"Oh. What's K-Pop?"

"K-Pop stands for Korean pop bands. You remember Korea - the country that kicked your ass in the coronavirus response. My favorite K-Pop band is Blackpink."

"Now I sort of remember. Didn't these K-Pop people and their followers screw up the attendance at my Tulsa rally?"

"They sure did. All of them pitched in when I made the request."

"Do you have all of their records?"

"Records? This is not the Stone Age, dad. Pretty much everything is done through TikTok. I, and all my friends, couldn't live without TikTok."

"Well, son, you're going to have to. I'm going to ban TikTok from operating in the U.S. and there's nothing to be done about it."

"Dad, did I mention my big writing assignment for this semester at school? We have to pick one person in our family and write about them in great detail. I was thinking about picking you. And Aunt Maryanne and Cousin Mary have agreed to help me. Now, remind me what you were saying about TikTok?"

"Great social media platform."

Pillow Talk

(Mike Lindell, founder and CEO of My Pillow, Inc., enters the Oval Office.)

"Mike, how good to see you. Come on in."

"The pleasure is all mine, Mr. President. When you called me in Minnesota and said you needed to see me, I jumped on the first plane to DC. Couldn't get a darn head pillow on the plane, though. What is it that's so urgent?"

"Well, Mike, you know how much I appreciate the humongous financial contributions you've made to my campaign. So I thought the least I could do is return the favor in any way I can. And this time, it concerns your business - My Pillow. The better that My Pillow does financially, the more money you can bribe me with, so this is win-win. OK?"

"Gotcha, Mr. President. You might not wear a cross on your chest when you appear in front of millions on TV, as I do, but we're still two peas in a pod. And you know, sir, I still thank the good lord Jesus that I found that marketing firm all those years ago that came up with the cross wearing idea. Simply brilliant. But what's the problem?"

"It's that new My Pillow you sent me."

"The new deluxe model that we're rolling out nationally as our #1 promotion? The pillow I sent you six weeks ago?"

"Well, first of all, I only got it two weeks ago. Damn mail is so slow these days. But more importantly, I have not had a single good night's sleep on that pillow. Tossing, turning, flipping it over, sore neck in the morning - it's awful."

"I'm very sorry to hear that, sir, and I agree that we definitely need to reformulate that pillow before my company goes bankrupt. But what to do?"

"You're in luck, Mike, because I have the perfect solution for you to use and promote, even before you do any tests on actual people. There's a poisonous extract of the oleander plant called oleandrin. It would make a perfect stuffing for a deluxe pillow. And there's a failsafe good sleep mechanism built in. If the sleeper still tosses and turns, they might end up eating some of the stuffing and then they really fall asleep."

"What a brilliant idea, sir. Any idea where I can lay my good, pious christian hands on this oleandrin stuff?"

"You get it from a company called Phoenix Biotechnology. They're reliable - Jared owns 40%."

"But what do I do with all this oleandrin stuff if it isn't actually a cure all for pillows?"

"Don't worry. I'm sure I can think of some alternative use."

(The meeting ends. Mike Lindell exits the Oval Office, just as Dr. Stella Immanuel - the new chief medical member of the Coronavirus Task Force - enters to update the President on the latest in COVID-19 therapeutics research.)

The Interview

(The President and the Chronicler-in-Chief of the Oh Daddy Chronicles arrive in the Rose Garden of the White House. The President offers his hand for a handshake and is met by an elbow bump from the Chronicler. Let the fun begin.)

"First, I would like to say, Mr. President, that it is an honor to be here. I can't tell you how many members of the Oh Daddy Chronicles Community really appreciate this."

"My pleasure. I'm sure they're all pretty special people to read all the wacky stuff you put out."

"That's just it. When I said that I couldn't tell you how many ODCC members really appreciate your coming here, it's because I actually have no idea how many members still read any of this."

"Well, I'm sure they'll read this one ."

"Hopefully. You know, sir, that your title and my title are almost interchangeable."

"What do you mean?"

"Well, if you use only the first initial of the first word of the title, we're both "C.-in-Chief." How cool! Maybe we should actually swap roles for a while, sort of like the "Prince and the Pauper."

"I don't think that would work. You have no idea how to be Commander-in-Chief."

"Don't be so sure. I've been watching you for 3 1/2 years showing the world how to have no idea how to be Commander-in-Chief."

"Clever little bugger, you are. On the other hand, I can't write worth a shit. So maybe I could impersonate you, after all."

"Good one, sir."

(Just then, the Chronicler-in-Chief lets out a huge, powerful sneeze.)

"Sorry, sir, rose allergies."

"Did anything get on me?"

"From the looks of your suit, sir, I'd say it was a direct hit. I did suggest that we wear masks, but you refused."

"Whatever, let's start the interview."

"Of course. Perhaps we can start with some personal matters to allow our members to get a feel for the real Donald Trump. Would that be all right?"

"Of course. Good idea."

"Tell us how you felt when Mrs. Trump first compared your body odor to that of her dear Uncle Slobodan, the pig farmer from Zagorje ob Savi."

"Didn't bother me at all. At least not at first. I had never met the man and I knew how fond Melania was of him. So I guess I took it as a compliment."

"But that changed?"

"Hell yes, it changed. Uncle Slobodan came for a one month visit to the White House. You might have seen him a few times - a guy walking around wearing bib overalls, chewing tobacco, not able to speak much English. It took me a while, but I was finally able to distinguish him from the other Trumpers that like to hang around. Anyway, geez that guy stunk! Once he left, the entire East Wing had to be fumigated. I even had the Secret Service set up a cot in the White House bunker for a week so I could breathe."

"Does it bother you that Barron speaks with a Slovenian accent?"

"Who?"

"Your son Barron."

"Oh him. Nah, it doesn't bother me. He can speak with any accent he wants. Melania rarely lets me see him anyway."

"You're well known, of course, for your love of tweeting. When did this fascination begin?"

"I guess it was shortly after Twitter started operations in 2006."

"And how did you find out about it so quickly?"

"Everyone was always saying to me: "twit! twit! twit!" I heard it as: "tweet! tweet! tweet!" So I did."

"Speaking of Twitter, as you know, their mascot is a blue bird. There is currently a shareholder movement to change the mascot to a black magpie in support of Black Birds Matter. How do you feel about that?"

"It would be a disgrace to our heritage and our history. Some very brave Americans have tweeted under the watchful eye of that blue bird - Abraham Lincoln, Antonin Scalia, George Patton, Harry Potter. I will not stand idly by and witness the humiliation done to these powerful Americans. In fact, I am prepared to sign an Executive Order requiring that all tweets made under the banner of the black magpie carry a warning saying: "This tweet is from a twit.""

"You seem to have a strong attraction to what is called a Newton's Cradle."

"A what?"

"Newton's Cradle. You know - a contraption with five balls whereby pulling one ball to the side and letting it bang into the others causes the ball on the opposite side to swing."

"Ahh. A ball swinging thingy. Why didn't you use the technical name?"

"Sorry. My bad. So how did you come upon this "thing" for a ball swinging thingy?"

"Well, it goes back to my childhood. My older brother Fred had one, but wouldn't let me play with it. I asked my father if I could have one of my own. He refused, saying it was too complicated for me. I resolved that one day I would get one of my own. I did. After two years of effort, I had mastered it. Boy, was dad proud. Unfortunately, Fred was already dead."

"Speaking of your father, your niece Mary Trump has published a book entitled "Too Much and Never Enough," in which she paints a rather unflattering portrait of your father - mean, nasty, insensitive, uncaring, manipulative, domineering. Would you care to comment?"

"Like father, like son."

"Do you have a favorite TV show?"

"I certainly do. It's Fox & Friends."

"What about a favorite fictionalized TV show, like a drama or comedy?"

"Fox & Friends."

"You've received criticism for pulling out of the WHO in the middle of a pandemic, that you pulled out too soon. How do you respond to that?"

"I have a long personal history of pulling out too soon. Just ask Melania."

"In the general topic of the pandemic, Dr. Anthony Fauci has come to be one of the most beloved and respected people in the United States. Yet you seem rather ambivalent towards him. Can you explain this?"

"I can. First of all, I think Tony's a great guy. And he's really smart, although smart people don't know everything. When I needed someone to fix my ball swinging thingy, for example, I didn't even consider asking Tony. I turned to Rudy, who might be as crazy as a sprayed cockroach, but he can get things done."

"Yes, but what is it in particular about Dr. Fauci that you don't like?"

"He's short. I just can't look up to short people."

"But you do look up to Vladimir Putin and he is the same height as Dr. Fauci - 5' 7"."

"Maybe, but Tony doesn't wear those super high platform heels like Vladimir. Looks stunning in that slinky red dress."

"Who do you consider to be the real heavyweight in your Cabinet?"

"That's a tough one. I sure as hell wouldn't want to be standing between Bill Barr and the shrimp cocktail when they open the White House buffet at 11:00. Then again, I've seen whole black forest cakes disappear in an instant when Pompeo is in the neighborhood. I guess he's not a fan of the Black Forest Cakes Matter Movement. So I'm just going to have to rate that one a toss-up."

"You meet with Senate Majority Leader Mitch McConnell from time to time."

"I do. Great guy, Mitch."

"Could you tell our members how it is that you can talk with him in person, face-to-face, without cracking up into hysterical laughter when you look at his gelatinous slab of neck flubber, his reptilian throat flesh that gobbles up babies, his ravenous blubbery abyss of corruption, his trademark turkey wattle chin? How do you keep a straight face?"

"Toughest part of the job."

"Many past Presidents have given us oratory that have inspired the nation and, indeed, the entire world. Would it be all right if I read just a few?"

"Of course. Read away."

"George Washington - "Associate with men of good quality if you esteem your own reputation, for it is better to be alone than in bad company.""

"I like that. I'd share it with my friends if I had any. Continue."

"Franklin D. Roosevelt - "We have always held to the hope, the belief, the conviction that there is a better life, a better world, beyond the horizon.""

"I'm perfectly happy with the one I have now. Continue."

"George W. Bush - "Leadership to me means duty, honor, country. It means character, and it means listening from time to time.""

"Does singing in the shower count? Any more quotes?"

"Last one. George H. W. Bush - "I do not like broccoli. And I haven't liked it since I was a little kid and my mother made me eat it. And I'm President of the United States and I'm not going to eat any more broccoli.""

"Inspiring. The President can do whatever he wants."

"What sage words would you leave for posterity, Mr. President?"

"Fuck 'em!"

"A few of our members gave me questions to ask you. Would that be all right?"

"Sure. I doubt they're any dumber than yours."

"Yes, well, the first is from Petrus. He asks "When mugging for the camera, have you ever bitten your tongue?""

"Tell Petrus that I have been told many times to bite my tongue, but I never have and never will."

"The next is from Josephine. She wonders if you wear Depends. With all the shit that comes out of your mouth it must surely flow backwards from time to time."

"Tell the bitch I refuse to answer such a crappy question. And you know, I'm almost never wrong, but this might be one of those rare times. These member questions *are* dumber than yours. Any more of them?"

"A few more. Geyser from the Finnish chapter of the ODCC wishes to know what you would do if your buddy Vladimir invaded Finland and confiscated all property there owned by Americans."

"This Geyser person is obviously uninformed. Everyone knows that Finland is already part of Russia. But if Vladimir confiscated American property, he would give half to the Trump Organization pursuant to the Salmiakki Treaty we signed two years ago."

"One of our founding members - Donatello - has three questions. First, he'd like to know how Mrs. Trump likes living in the White House compared with Trump Tower."

"Well, at Trump Tower, we were on separate floors. At the White House, Melania has a couple of rooms near mine. So I guess she prefers Trump Tower."

"His second question relates to naps. He'd like to know how many naps you take on a daily basis."

"Now that's an interesting question. Let's see. There's the Daily National Security Briefing, the daily coronavirus update, and occasionally Peter Navarro comes in with one of his 87-page memos. So I guess it's two or three naps a day."

"Finally, Donatello wishes to know if you plan to attend Joe Biden's inauguration."

"You really have some smart asses in your group. Tell me where this guy lives so I can have Kimberly Gargoyle scream outside his window."

"Just one more. Roberto would like to know which episode of the Oh Daddy Chronicles is your favorite."

"Have you read the episode called "Book Worm?"

"Read it? Of course, I wrote it."

"Then you should know that I read with my ears. Let me know when your Chronicles is available as an audio book. Maybe I could answer your question then."

"I think that's about it, sir. I would like to thank you, on behalf of the entire Oh Daddy Chronicles Community, for taking the time to chat with us today. Do you have any message you wish to share with us?"

"I do. I'd like to say how much I admire your group for putting up with all the drivel you write. And, most importantly, "Long Live the Chronicles!"

(The interview ends. The Chronicler-in-Chief leaves the Rose Garden, having pocketed a pen with the Presidential insignia while the President's attention was distracted by an elbow bump.)

I Lost My Cupcake

(Counselor to the President, Kellyanne Conway, enters the Oval Office.)

"Come in, Kellyanne. Have a seat. You said there was something you needed to see me about."

"Here, Mr. President." (Kellyanne hands the President a piece of paper with one short typewritten paragraph and her signature.)

"Umm, would you mind giving me the oral version, please?"

"I quit. I am resigning. Effective September 1."

"What? Holy shit! You can't do that! Who's going to take the idiotic crap I say and turn it into something only half-idiotic? Who's going to convince people that standing in line to vote during the Chinese virus pandemic is no different from standing in line to get a chocolate ganache cupcake from Georgetown Cupcakes? Who's going to present alternative facts to the media? Who's going to wear more make-up than I do? Who? Who? Who?"

"Calm down, sir. Here are some tissues."

"Can I bribe you to stay? How about a Georgetown Cupcakes franchise of your own? A two-hour scarf fashion consultation with Dr. Birx? You get first dibs at the White House lunch buffet dessert table before fatso Pompeo is allowed to go there? Your own dedicated supply of hydroxychloroquine? I can even move your office further away from the assistant dweeb-in-chief, Jared Kushner. What do you say?"

"I'm afraid not, sir. I've already turned down some pretty amazing job offers."

"Such as?"

"Well, the Brazilian Senate offered to make me President of Brazil."

"Whatever for?"

"They're having almost as difficult a time with the coronavirus as we are. It is well established that countries with women leaders have fared the best in the pandemic."

"But you can't be the President of Brazil."

"I can't? Why not?"

"Because you don't speak Spanish."

"And that's not the only job offer I've gotten. I've been asked to head the NAMOTTIC."

"The what?"

"The NAMOTTIC - National Association of Microwave Ovens That Turn Into Cameras. They're looking into new facial recognition technology. Twitching your nose means one minute; closing one eye means two minutes; yawning means "surprise me." Very exciting stuff, but I turned down the offer."

(Ed. note - In March 2017, Kellyanne Conway claimed that surveillance could be done with microwave ovens that turn into cameras.)

"But why? Why are you leaving?"

"As you know, sir, George and I have four children."

"I sure as hell hope they got all of their jeans from you and not from that scumbag husband of yours."

"We have three daughters and one son, so 75% of their jeans come from me. But that's not the point. Our eldest daughter, especially, needs more of my attention. All of my time must be devoted to my four biological children. I simply can no longer take care of a fifth."

"But Kellyanne, you can't just leave me holding the bag like this. How am I going to find someone to replace you?"

"You don't have to, sir. I've already done that. My replacement is waiting in the hallway, and you already know her... Come on in, Stella."

(Dr. Stella Immanuel enters the Oval Office, her medicinal snake Reggie wrapped around her shoulders.)

Acceptance Speech

"I want to welcome all the billions of you out there who are watching me right now as I give my acceptance speech for the nomination of the Republican Party for Dictator, er I mean, President of the United States. As everyone can see, this is the biggest acceptance speech crowd in acceptance speech history. Its ratings are so high that Mr. Nielsen had to bring his whole family with him to count everybody. And I want to thank my technical staff who figured out how to program Nielsen to count by twos.

"As we look to the next four years, we should take stock of what has happened in the last four years. And, of course, all that really matters is, indeed, the stock market.

"In the area of public health, my Administration (that means me) has made great strides to reduce the number of Americans with diabetes, obesity, and cardiovascular disease. At last count, I have almost single-handedly dropped that number by around 178,000. Let's see Sleepy Joe top that!

"And I will not be ignoring the rapidly disappearing coronavirus. My Administration will target all three areas that the public health dicks (except for Deborah) talk about. We'll make testing easier so everyone can pass them. Maybe we can shine one of those purple fluorescent lights inside a person's mouth and see if any coronaviruses show up. For tracing, we'll distribute lots and lots of tracing paper and I'll produce a podcast on the best way to trace all sorts of things - animals, golf courses, money. And we'll shorten the quarantine and isolation period to two days so people will like it better. I'll make an Executive Order requiring the cable companies to make only Fox News and OANN available in all quarantine facilities.

"When I took office, the National Stockpile was almost completely empty of the things this country needs. But no longer. In my second term, I will invoke the Defense Production Act for the mass production of statues of Confederate generals. And all of them will be anchored ten feet into the ground to make them topple proof. And, for good measure, I'll rename my hometown. Won't be called Queens anymore - for obvious reasons. We need a real man's name. Something like "Trumpsylvania," to honor all the blood I've sucked out of the spirit of this country.

"Before I talk about the economy, I want to make a short digression for a powerful, strong, unbelievable announcement. Most of you know that one of the greatest American patriots of our time, someone to whom I have often looked for advice and will do so in the future, someone intimately knowledgeable about the national security ramifications of pizza, is, of course, Q. Until now, no one other than Q himself knew who he was. Hence, he has been referred to as QAnon. No longer. I will reveal right now the true identity of Q. He is with me here in the White House. Come on out."

(At that, Paul Rubenfeld, better known as Pee-wee Herman, flashes across the TV screen.)

"Turning to the economy. I single-handedly took the greatest economy in the history of the world and destroyed it. Who better to build it back up than the person who broke it? You need to understand that the economy cannot be separated from the virus. So anyone who needs a job, can get a test. Anyone who wants a job, can get a test. Anyone who needs an extra $600 per week, can get a test. Anyone who watches Fox News, can get a test. Anyone who comes anywhere near me *has* to get a test.

"Our country has seen much civil unrest in the last year. This will not continue in my second term. Municipalities will be forced to crack down powerfully on protestors or they will lose key Federal assistance on painting fire hydrants, fixing sidewalk cracks, and issuing jaywalking tickets. So there!

"Finally, we cannot ignore international relationships. Even though everyone says I am too cozy with Putin, I will make it a priority in my second term to push him to finally grant Finland its independence. And if Uruguay wants to join South America, why shouldn't they be allowed to? If the Low countries of Europe aspire to raise themselves up, we'll be there to help. And I don't want to hear anyone complain about what I have done to NATO. I have personally done more to bring all of the NATO countries together (except for the U.S.) in their mutual dislike and ridicule of me than any President since James Garfield.

"In closing, I ask you: "Are you worse off today than you were four years ago?" For those of you pumping your fist into the air and going "Yeah, Yeah, Yeah," then just imagine how excited you'll be when I ask you the same question four years from now.

"God bless America and God bless Donald Trump."

NATO

(At his campaign speech in New Hampshire on August 28, the President asked reporters to call NATO Secretary General and former Norwegian Prime Minister Jens Stoltenberg to solicit praise for the President. One intrepid reporter took him up on the suggestion.)

(The Oval Office administrative assistant announces the arrival of the "reporter.")

"Come in and have a seat. I'm glad to see that someone has the balls to call that Dutch guy with me."

"Aren't we calling NATO Secretary General Jens Stoltenberg?"

"Sure, whatever his name is."

"But Mr. Stoltenberg is from Norway, not The Netherlands."

"Oh. Whatever. Would you like a Danish pastry? I can have some brought in from the kitchen. And you don't have to pay for it - no Dutch treat." (The President chortles at his way with words.)

"No thank you, sir. Perhaps we could make the call? I have a deadline to meet. My article needs to make it into tonight's edition so that the papers can be delivered by the Postal Service by Tuesday next week."

"Hey, Oval Office administrative assistant, get me the head of NATO on the phone."

"Pierre Serafin speaking. How may I help you?" (The voice speaks English with a heavy French accent.)

"This is President Donald Trump. I am in the Oval Office at the White House with Mr. Reporter. Are you the head of NATO?"

"Indeed I am, sir. And it is most welcome that I get to speak with the head honcho."

"I'd like Mr. Reporter here to hear all the great things you have to say about me and my accomplishments."

"I would be most happy to do so, sir. There are so many I don't know where to begin. Perhaps I start with the slave labor wages you pay to so many of your employees. Then there is the lack of paid childcare leave. No sick days allowed. How about the bribes paid to local officials for zoning variations? And I save the best for last - forcing employees to work in conditions that are in close proximity to those cancer causing windmills."

"Wait. Are you sure you're the head of NATO?"

"Yes, I am sure."

"But what about that other guy?" (Trump looks to Mr. Reporter for help.) "Yeah, that Jens Stoltenberg guy."

"Ah. Mr. Stoltenberg is the Secretary General of the other NATO - North Atlantic Treaty Organization."

"Then what is your NATO?"

"Nations Against the Trump Organization."

(The President ends the call and summons the Oval Office administrative assistant.)

"That was the wrong NATO. Try again."

"Hello. How can I help to make your day as spiritually fulfilling as possible?"

"Huh? Well you can start by connecting me with the head of NATO."

"Certainly, my friend and companion on our shared journey on this lovely planet."

(Trump to Mr. Reporter) "I had no idea the cutback in our support for NATO would have such far reaching personnel effects."

"Good afternoon, fellow traveler. This is Melissa Podcast, head of NATO. It's such a pleasure to speak with you. And your name is?"

"This is Donald Trump, President of the United States and I've got Mr. Reporter with me."

"Oh dear, I am so sorry about your multiple mental afflictions. But I am overjoyed that you have decided to reach out to the healing power of New Age Turtles. You will never look back."

(The President is speechless and Mr. Reporter tries to stifle a laugh.)

"Usually in these cases, I assign the patient to one of our NATO therapists, but for you, I will handle your case myself. Here's how we will proceed. Please ask one of your staff to purchase a medium sized turtle, preferably green. You will need to caress the turtle three times daily for two weeks, say 10 minutes per caress. Download my eBook entitled "The Role of New Age Turtles in Mental Health" and commit it to memory. I'll need to have an in-person session with you here in Oregon. After that, we should be able to manage by tele-medicine."

(The President remains speechless. Mr. Reporter speaks up.)

"Excuse me, Ms. Podcast, what do your initials "NATO" stand for?"

"Why, they stand for New Age Turtles Organization."

"Thank you, but I think we reached the wrong NATO."

(The President tries one last time.)

"Hey, Oval Office administrative assistant, would you get me the real NATO on the phone this time?"

"Good afternoon. NATO headquarters."

"I'd like to speak with Jens Stoltenberg."

"Certainly, sir. I'll connect you."

"Jissn Stolibg speing."

"Who? You sound like you have a hot potato in your mouth."

"Sorry. I was trying out my Danish impersonation.. This is Jens Stoltenberg, Secretary General of NATO. With whom do I have the pleasure of speaking?"

"This is Donald Trump, President of the United States. With me is..."

(A loud thwack is heard, almost as if a telephone receiver had been slammed down.)

The Meeting

(Door to Oval Office opens and in walks New York governor Andrew Cuomo, carrying a briefcase and a large bag with steam emerging from the top.)

"Andrew, welcome, please have a seat. And it looks like you brought what I asked for."

"Well, sort of. I know you made it very clear that you wished to meet with me solely as an excuse to taste my mom's secret tomato sauce recipe, right?"

"I did indeed. Why else would I lower myself to meet with you? Your ratings are way lower than mine. Mine are huge. Mine are beautiful. Mine are fantastic. Mine are unbelievable. What are yours?"

"Actually, I have no idea. I have more important things demanding my attention, right?"

"What??? What could be more important? You know, I just don't understand intelligent, thoughtful, caring, dedicated people like you. It's like you're from a different planet. Same with Obama. Anyway, enough of that. Let's eat."

(White House butler, a Mexican immigrant, prepares the table and puts the spaghetti and meatballs on two plates. Trump grabs the larger one for himself and starts to wolf - no relation to Blitzer- his food down.)

"Yuck!!! This is disgusting!" (Trump says as he inhales his tomato sauced spaghetti using two forks instead of a fork and spoon.) "If this is your mother's legendary tomato sauce recipe, then she's a total piece of shit!"

"I tried to tell you, Mr. President, before you went off on your ratings, that this is not my mother's recipe, it's mine, right? Had you been watching my brother Chris on CNN's Prime Time with Chris Cuomo a couple of weeks ago, you would have learned that Chris was the culinary talent among the siblings and mom gave the recipe to him. Whenever my daughters come for Sunday dinner, they push my spaghetti and meatballs around on the plate and then head out for Chinese takeout. You might also have learned other useful things had you paid attention to CNN rather than Fox News, right?"

(Trump calls in Vice President Pence, National Security Advisor Robert O'Brien, Dr. Deborah Birx - scarf and all -, Dr. Anthony Fauci, President of the Tomato Sauce of America Society Giuseppe Sauceatoni, The Flying Spaghetti Monster, and the White House executive chef.)

(Trump is irate.)

"Why didn't someone advise me that this tomato sauce is actually a clear and present danger to anyone who eats it? And the meatballs are also kind of squishy. And the spaghetti is rubbery. I demand an explanation!"

"I did a tasting three days ago, sir, and told Mr. Navarro. I believe he wrote a 73 page memo. Weren't you briefed on it?" (said the White House executive chef)

"Nobodya aska mea." (said Giuseppe Sauceatoni)

"I warned you two weeks ago that we needed a lot more testing." (said the esteemed Dr. Fauci, who, by way of his Italian heritage is one of the leading experts in tomato sauce as well as infectious diseases.)

"It really depends on the conditions present locally. I warned you of that three weeks ago." (said scarf swinging Dr. Birx)

"We advised you of this insidious culinary threat five weeks ago, as soon as we saw what was happening in Italy. And our response time was extremely fast because you had the foresight to use the funds freed up from disbanding the National Security Council Pandemic Response Team to set up a new Tomato Sauce Global Surveillance Network" (said National Security Advisor O'Brien)

"Under your leadership, Mr. President, we actually identified the threat about two months ago. Our agents in China, tasked with monitoring developments in Chinese noodle labs, saw this coming, in particular from one noodle lab in Wuhan. We all advised you of the threat. Under your forceful and determined leadership and direction, we all did nothing." (said the Vice President who then rose from his knees)

(Notably absent from the meeting was The Flying Spaghetti Monster - The Sauce Be Upon Him. His whereabouts were unknown because He is invisible.)

"Excuses, excuses, excuses. That's all I get is excuses. Find me at least five people/organizations to blame. The usual suspects - Pelosi (she's Italian), Democrats, China (they invented noodles), Soros (I bet he eats tomatoes), the WFO (World Food Organization). And get Rudy involved - he has connections in the Italian underworld. Now get the hell out of here - all of you. But not you, Andrew. We haven't eaten yet."

(Only Trump and Cuomo are left, sitting at the table.)

"Well, Andrew. I really worked up an appetite. How about some Chinese take-out?"

(They both start with the egg rolls...)

The Meeting Ends

(Trump and Governor Cuomo put the finishing touches to a most satisfying meal of Chinese take-out. Trump lets out a huge burp and fart, but Cuomo pretends not to notice. They both eagerly latch on to their respective fortune cookies.)

"So Mr. President, do you believe in fortune cookies? That what they say really will come true?"

"Of course, I do. It would be inconsistent with my track record of believing in pseudoscience if I didn't. Let's see what mine says."

"So what does it say, Mr. President?'

"When the cow comes home from its pasture in the high mountain Alpine snows and sees its shadow on the black raven, then peace will descend on the land of its ancestors."

"Wow. Heavy duty."

"And what about yours?" What does it say?"

(Cuomo opens his fortune cookie and reads it to himself. A shitty grin comes across his face.)

"I don't want to read it out loud, Mr. President."

"Well then, give it here and I'll read it."

(Trump takes the fortune cookie, reads it, and has a heart attack.)

(Cuomo calls for help and then flies back to New York.)

(In the evening, the janitor cleaning the Oval Office (a Mexican immigrant) finds a small rectangular piece of paper near the table where the two had their Chinese take-out. Curious, he opens the paper and reads: "Biden will withdraw. You will be the nominee of the Democratic Party." The janitor smiles and tucks the paper into his shirt pocket.)

.

All Recovered

(The door to the Oval Office opens and in steps White House press secretary Kayleigh McEnany.)

"Good morning, Mr. President. I am so glad to see you fully recovered and resolutely back at work behind the Resolute Desk. And, my oh my, your staff even remembered to bring back your favorite ball swinging thingy that you insisted on taking with you to Walter Reed as your sleep toy."

"They sure did. I think I have finally found a real keeper in this Mark Meadows guy. What is he, my 17th chief of staff?"

(Kayleigh decides it is prudent to just ignore the question.)

"So, Mr. President, did the doctors ever find the reason for the heart attack?"

(Trump has an uncomfortable look on his face. Meanwhile, the Mexican immigrant janitor, doing some last minute tidying up, has an expression on his face that no one can figure out.)

"Not really. They said it was probably the result of some external shock that overwhelmed my system. Maybe some nightmare fake news. Either that or hydroxychloroquine cardiotoxicity presenting as a rapidly evolving biventricular cardiomyopathy."

"Well, you're really pretty lucky. The surgery took 37 hours."

"37 hours?!? That's impossible. No heart surgery can take that long. Who do the surgeons think they are - the U.S. Senate? Or were they trying to imitate my Coronavirus Task Force news conferences?"

"Actually, Mr. President, it's kind of like when my father used to go to the local barbershop (before they all went out of business)."

"Huh? Is this one of those alternative facts thingies you picked up from Kellyanne?"

"No, Mr. President, let me explain. My father was, for the most part, bald. All of us in the family expected his trips to the barber would be very short. But he was always there for around two hours in the barber chair. Not 37 hours, but still pretty darn long for a haircut."

"Why so long? It can't take that long to cut or fix his hair."

"You're right. It didn't. Most of that time was spent trying to find it."

"I like that story. Cute. Not beautiful, but close enough. But what does that have to do with my surgery?"

(Kayleigh decides it is prudent to just ignore the question.)

"Who has been filling in while I have been away?"

"No one can replace you, sir, of course."

(Trump beams.)

"But Vice President Pence has stepped in and done a great job."

(The beam diminishes.)

"Everyone has remarked about how much the Vice President has gotten things done."

(The beam turns into a scowl.)

"Tell that little white haired, silver tongued ass licker that he either gets his butt in here soon or I'll order him to have a private two person only dinner with that hot Hispanic housemaid who does the

2nd floor at Mar a Lago. I'm the President, after all, and I have total authority - total."

(Kayleigh starts to leave, but a fuming Trump calls her back.)

"Before you go, let's watch a little Fox News."

(Kayleigh turns on the television just in time for them to see the breaking news.)

"At 10:15 this morning, former Vice President Joe Biden announced that he has withdrawn his candidacy for the Presidency of the United States. He claims that it was all a misunderstanding - he thought he was running for dog catcher. In the ensuing turmoil, the entire Democratic National Committee, former Presidents Bill Clinton and Barack Obama, Her Royal Highness the Queen of England, and the entire Cabinet of Donald Trump practically begged New York governor Andrew Cuomo to accept the nomination of his party for the Presidency of the United States. He accepted, to the massive relief of a grateful world. He then immediately introduced his running mate - Michelle Obama."

(On split screens: 1). Trump crumples to the floor with a massive heart attack. 2). Cuomo is on the phone with Mr. Wang of Chinese Happy Buddha restaurant of K Street thanking him for the special fortune cookie he prepared.)

(Snuzzlepuff bursts into the Oval Office, sees the President crumpled on the floor, and proclaims for all to hear: "OH DADDY!"

* *

EPILOGUE

The Oh Daddy Chronicles is now brought to an end. It chronicled the life of a family, together with their interactions with others, during the most challenging and downright weird time in the lives of all of us. For most, those times brought out the best in us. For a few, well, that didn't happen.

Time passed. Life provided its normal twists and turns. Here is what happened to some of the characters in this chronicle.

Donald Trump ("Daddykins")

Donald Trump never fully recovered from the second massive heart attack. He ended up sleeping almost 18 hours a day and came to be known as "Sleepy Donald." He did not run for reelection. He spent his remaining years in a corner suite of rooms on the fourth floor of Mar a Lago, watching old reruns of The Rocky and Bullwinkle Show and playing with his cherished ball swinging thingy. The bookshelves were lined not with books, but rather with an assortment of different colored Lysol bottles. Eventually, no one came to visit, not even the hot Hispanic maid responsible for the Mar a Lago second floor. He died, alone, at the age of 82, from an overdose of hydroxychloroquine. Sad.

Ivanka Trump ("Snuzzlepuff")

Ivanka sort of drifted off out of the spotlight. When Jared spent increasing amounts of time trying to solve the toothpaste problem, she decided she'd had enough and divorced him, citing irreconcilable differences - she was intelligent, he was an idiot; she was beautiful, he was dweebie. Following Melania's divorce, the two of them (Ivanka and Melania) moved to California and were joined in a same sex union. Happily ever after.

Donald Trump Jr. ("Danko")

Simply put, Don Jr. was caught. His role as chief instigator of the "Liberate" protests was uncovered. Those socially un-distanced protests were later estimated to have caused 547 additional COVID-19 deaths. Don Jr. was convicted of involuntary manslaughter for every one of them. Because of his family's influence, he was able to get himself placed in a cell with his "uncles" - Paul Manafort and Roger Stone. Isn't life sweet.

Jared Kushner

Ah, Jared. Truth be told, no one really knows what became of him. After his devastating divorce from Ivanka (devastating to him; perhaps not so devastating to her), he seemed to simply vanish. At first, people started looking for him. But after about eight minutes, they stopped, realizing that nobody actually cared. Some persistent rumors floated around that Jared was seen flipping burgers at one of Chris Christie's Chris's Chris Steakhouses, resurrected from the ashes of the coronavirus economic meltdown by way of a $60 million small business loan from the Paycheck Protection Program (PPP), but that rumor was never confirmed. So it goes.

Melania Trump

Melania Trump became increasingly disgusted with the smell emanating from her husband. She finally resorted to using clothes pins to squeeze her nostrils closed in a desperate attempt to shut out the smell that reminded her so much of her Uncle Slobodan, the pig farmer from Zagorje ob Savi. But when Jared's Project Clothes Pin Airbridge, bringing desperately needed nostril personal protective equipment from Bophuthatswana shut down, Melania had no choice but to divorce her husband. She and Ivanka eventually moved to California where they were joined in a same sex union. Melania engaged the services of a speech coach and now sounds like a cross between a Brooklyn plumber and Christiane Amanpour.

Andrew Cuomo

Andrew Cuomo became the 46th President of the United States, defeating then Vice President Mike Pence in a landslide. He served, along with his Vice President Michelle Obama, for eight glorious years, during which time the United States began the long climb of regaining its once lofty position in the world that had been so tragically squandered. The process was finally completed during the administration of the 47th President of the United States – Michelle Obama.

The Cuomo administration was almost completely scandal free. The only minor blemish began innocently enough. Andrew Cuomo and family, his brother Chris Cuomo and family, along with the Obamas decided to invite a reporter to one of their regular Sunday spaghetti and meatball dinners. By this time, Chris Cuomo had introduced Mama Cuomo's famous secret tomato sauce recipe to the nation in a successful commercial venture that eclipsed even Newman's Own. The reporter heard Vice President Obama exclaiming how delicious the tomato sauce was and reported this on CNN. Republicans in Congress were furious when they discovered that the State Unemployment Office cafeteria in Nebraska began serving Mama Cuomo's Secret Tomato Sauce. They claimed a violation of the Domestic Emoluments Clause of the U.S. Constitution (Article II, Section 1, Paragraph 7) and clamored for impeachment. Two days later, after doing the math, they dropped the impeachment idea when it was pointed out to them that, with only three Republican members of the House of Representatives and only two Republican Senators, impeachment and removal from office were a tad unlikely.

Joe Biden

Former Vice President Joe Biden became an even more beloved figure in American politics after his judicious decision not to run for the Presidency. His insatiable appetite for self-sacrificing public service landed him a position in the Cuomo administration. He was appointed U.S. Ambassador to Ukraine.

Kellyanne Conway

Finally freed from the strain of covering for Donald Trump, Kellyanne and husband George moved to New Zealand. George became a successful sheep farmer. They lived on his ranch called The Lincoln Project Corral. Kellyanne saw the error of her previous ways and became communications director for Jacinda Ardern's progressive government. It is rumored that, once Kellyanne tossed aside her Halloween witch costume and mask, she began to take on a vague resemblance to Olivia Newton John.

Mike Pence

Vice President Pence became the nominee of the Republican party for the Presidency in the 2020 election. His loss was one for the history books. He received the grand total of zero electoral college votes. He later admitted that even he voted for Cuomo. The public humiliation changed his life. He got rid of all the Bibles in his house (took two large moving vans to do so), divorced his wife, and became an alcoholic and womanizer. He spent his last 25 years happier than he had ever been.

Mike Pompeo

As the Trump presidency neared its end, it became apparent that Secretary Pompeo was in deep yogurt and would be indicted on several counts. His pleas to the President for a full pardon initially fell on deaf ears, until the President was overheard saying: "I'd like you to do me a favor, though. I want your really nice, even nicer than mine, ball swinging thingy." Pompeo felt he had little choice and reluctantly surrendered this prized possession. He then retired to rural Kansas and opened a fly fishing school so he could wear one of those hats with all those weird little thingies hanging from it. Life never fails to amaze.

John Bolton

Having pissed off everyone he ever worked for, and having zero bombs dropped to show for it, John Bolton decided to pursue a childhood dream - facial hair. He realized that specialists in facial hair couture were a dime a dozen. So he created a fusion business in which he perfected a technique for growing caterpillars and other small creepies in the lush facial hair above the upper lip, which he trademarked as "Bolton's Swamp." All attempts by the President to drain it proved futile.

Nikki Haley

The Republican ticket of Pence/Kaur Randhawa suffered a historic defeat in the 2020 election. Nikki Haley's only consolation was that she received more write-in votes for President than Pence received in total. Following the election, she went totally ethnic, packed her bags, and moved to India. She went into business with her pen pal, Joshadaben Modi, obtaining the India franchise for "Fauci and Gupta Cook It Like It Is" restaurants. Her chapatis became world famous and soon became the symbol of chapati resistance movements for oppressed people around the world. (Ed. note – think of the chapati movement immediately preceding the Sepoy Rebellion of 1859.) Comfortable that she had finally found her true inner self, she opened a spiritual consulting practice on the side, charging 50,000 Indian rupees (about $650) an hour. Om.......

Dr. Anthony Fauci

When the pandemic was finally over, Dr. Fauci ended his media stint educating the public on the coronavirus. CNN's chief medical correspondent – Dr. Sanjay Gupta – made a similar decision. These two titans of the coronavirus battle opened a restaurant together in Laredo, Texas. It was an Italian/Indian fusion cuisine eatery called "Fauci and Gupta Cook It Like It Is." The breakfast menu was more traditional, with the most popular item being "Lox with the Docs." Fauci used tele-learning to get cooking lessons from Giuseppe Sauceatoni in Civita di Bagnoregio, while Sanjay got his tele-learning cooking lessons from Joshadaben Modi in Delhi.

Dr. Deborah Birx

Dr. Deborah Birx left a distinguished career in government service upon the inauguration of President Andrew Cuomo. She decided to try her fortune in the private sector, where she consulted with several pharmaceutical companies on vaccine development and immunological drug programs. This lucrative foray outside the Beltway was short-lived, however, when Macy's department store launched an investigation of why its inventory of Hermes scarves had plummeted without a concomitant increase in revenues. All roads led back to Rome. A grand jury returned an indictment and Dr. Birx entered a plea of nolo contendere. She was sentenced to serve five years as the personal physician of former president Donald Trump.

Dr. Sean Conley

After having his medical license revoked for "unorthodox" treatments, Dr. Conley resigned from the U.S. Navy. He and his family moved to the remote village of Knoydart in the Scottish highlands. It took him a while to adjust to the new pace of life. For example, he went to the local shop for a morning newspaper. The old lady shopkeeper asked him if he would be wantin' today's paper or be wantin' yesterday's paper. When he replied "today's paper," he was told that he need be comin' back tomorra. Eventually, he started what became a successful online education business teaching people how to acquire a dreadful, phony Scottish accent.

Betsy DeVos

During her time as Secretary of Education, Betsy Devos committed the entire billion dollar plus fortune she had inherited from her father into a scheme promoted by Don Jr. and Eric selling orange tinted facial care products. Despite such products being heavily promoted in all Trump Organization properties, the business idea was a colossal failure and Betsy was left penniless. She ended up getting a job as a part-time hall monitor in a Chicago inner city elementary school.

Slobodan Krajnc (Uncle Slobodan)

Uncle Slobodan returned to Slovenia from his White House visit to much fanfare. Having learned that being steeped in shit all day is actually a political advantage, he turned his attention to Slovenian electoral politics. Rising to the position of Parliamentary Speaker, he became best known for changing the traditional aye or nay vote to "yabba dabba doo" or "oink," which became the standard across Europe (except in the UK, of course, where they insisted on their centuries old tradition of "the tea is fine like it is" or "I say, it could use a bit more sugar, what?" Upon retirement, he returned to his pig farm in Zagorje ob Savi. Despite numerous requests, Donald Trump never came to visit.

Fu On Yu

Fu On Yu pursued a promising career in the national security apparatus until he succumbed to his life-long desire to be a stand-up comedian. His career really took off when he teamed up with former West Virginia senator Joe Manchin, who took the stage name Joe Manchu. The comedy duo of Fu Manchu, considered the modern day equivalent of Abbott and Costello, was perhaps best known for bestowing on Donald Trump his adopted Korean name of "Wun Dum Fuk."

Squishie

Following their chance encounter in the White House, Squishie and Attorney General Barr became good friends. With the help of seed capital provided by the Koch Brothers, Squishie and Barr opened several dance studios in the D.C. area, called "If Barr can do it..." They were so successful, they expanded their market coverage into the heartland, where they found particular success among non-college-educated white males wearing bib overalls and driving pick-up trucks with gun racks. The Squishie/Barr dance phenomenon caused a pronounced shift in political thinking that forever changed the political landscape in favor of the Democrats. What is now known as the Squishie/Barr blue shift can be traced to those innovative dance moves.

Giuseppe Sauceatoni

Giuseppe grew up in the beautiful village of Civita di Bagnoregio in the province of Lazio, in Italia. He and his four siblings worked in their papa's gelato shop. He learned about tomato sauce from his mom. He moved to the US at the age of 18 and lived there 25 years. He finally decided that it was in Lazio that he wanted to raise his family. So he moved back to his native village and opened a Chef Boyardee franchise.

The Mexican immigrant janitor

A rags to riches story. The American dream. The unnamed janitor who found the fortune cookie on the floor of the Oval Office kept the piece of paper. After Cuomo's eight years in office came to an end - mourned by much of the world - the janitor put the fortune cookie paper up for sale on eBay. He sold it for $42.7 million. He used the proceeds to purchase the now derelict Mar a Lago resort out of bankruptcy court and restored it to its former glory. When he met the hot Hispanic maid responsible for the second floor, it was love at first sight. They married. And, it turns out, she had brains as well as beauty because it was she who initiated the special guided tours of the suite of rooms in one of the corners of the fourth floor, where, if the tour group was lucky, they could catch a glimpse of The Donald yawning before falling back asleep.

Mr. Wang So Fun

Mr. Wang So Fun was the proprietor of the Chinese Happy Buddha restaurant on K St. His skill at custom made fortune cookies became widely known and he developed a sprawling national franchise. Eventually, the business was acquired by Starbucks and that is why you now see a large fortune cookie display in all Starbucks locations.

The Flying Spaghetti Monster (May the Sauce be Upon Him)

For those of you not familiar with the Flying Spaghetti Monster, I recommend a visit to Mr. Google. You will enjoy the trip. The FSM, simply put, is believed by many to be the Creator and Maintainer of the Universe. But, you might say, His Noodliness doesn't seem to have a role in this Chronicle. Ah, but remember that it was the especially tasty tomato sauce derived from a secret and treasured family recipe held by Matilda Cuomo (wife of the late Mario and mother of Maria, Margaret, Madeline, Andrew and Christopher) that initiated these fateful events. And who do you think gave this special tomato sauce recipe to beloved Matilda?.......... You guessed right.

SARS-CoV-2 (the coronavirus)

It took its toll. In suffering, in loss, in treasure, in terrible self-hair-cuts. Ultimately, it proved to be one of those viruses not very amenable to a robust vaccine so it could not be totally eliminated by science. Various therapeutics proved useful and turned the virus into a manageable nuisance. The most powerful of the therapeutics - a preventative actually - was a simple meal, taken once a week, of spaghetti and meatballs smothered in a particularly tasty tomato sauce made from a secret and treasured family recipe. When the power of the human spirit to act together to do what was necessary finally coalesced, the fate of the virus was a foregone conclusion. Let history not repeat itself.

* *

And so concludes the *Oh Daddy Chronicles*. Thank you for reading and May the Sauce be Upon You.